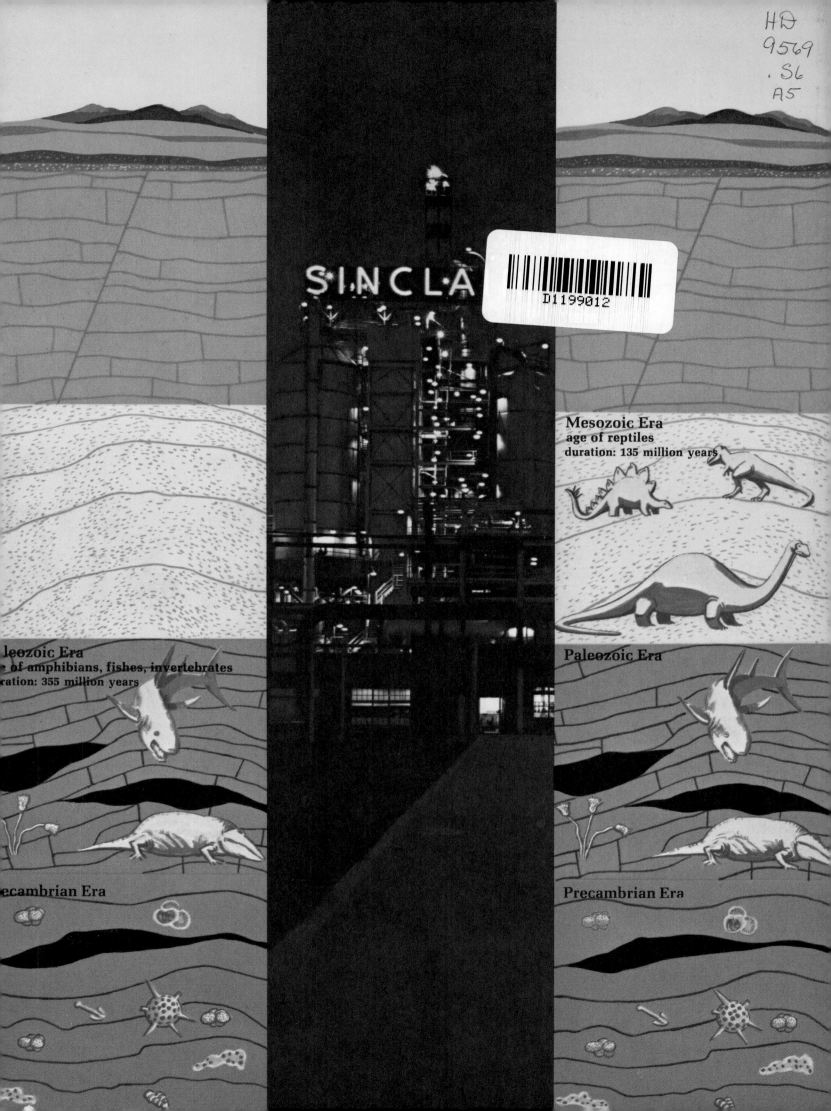

Mesozoic Era
age of reptiles
duration: 135 million years

Paleozoic Era
e of amphibians, fishes, invertebrates
ration: 355 million years

Paleozoic Era

ecambrian Era

Precambrian Era

Cenozoic Era
age of man and mammals
duration: 63 million years

Mesozoic Era

Paleozoic Era

Precambrian Era

Sinclair

50779

a great name in oil

Sinclair through fifty years

copyright © 1966 by Sinclair Oil Corporation
all rights reserved—printed in U.S.A.
Library of Congress catalog card number: 66-12042
published by F. W. Dodge Company/McGraw-Hill, Inc.
editorial consultant: Hartzell Spence
design consultant: Norman Jervis

The words *Sinclair* and *company* are used loosely in this volume. According to particular context, *Sinclair* may refer to the founder, the parent corporation, or to any or all of the operating subsidiaries.

a dedication

to Sinclair's 112,000 stockholders,
50,000 employees, dealers, suppliers
and 4,000,000 customers

*"In a brief span of years petroleum has altered man's way
of life throughout the world."*

The foregoing words are inscribed on the monument marking the site of the well that brought in the great Spindletop field in Texas, for all to read and ponder.

While never the largest or the most important company in this significant and eventful industry, Sinclair for 50 years now has been a great name in oil.

Sinclair has been a part of and an energetic contributor to this mighty work that has changed the world, that has lifted burdens from the laden backs of mankind, and given men and women a freedom of movement beyond even the visions of Leonardo da Vinci.

It has often been lamented that business men have no history. This anniversary book is not a corporate history in the conventional sense. Rather, we have here sought to give our friends an interesting, readable, accurate and candid account of a goodly company of men and women who have worked for half a century that the Sinclair organization might serve and, in serving well, might prosper.

In their work they have established and enjoyed a splendid fellowship. In their work they have grown a fierce loyalty to each other, and to that corporate entity that proudly flies the Sinclair banner.

Join us in the following pages through human tribulation and triumph, through brief despair and enduring achievement. And gaze with us into far horizons to those heights we plan and hope some day to scale and occupy.

Chairman of the Board
Chief Executive Officer

chapter 1:

fifty years of independence

With the Annual Meeting of 1966, the widely-ramified petroleum operations emblazoned with the Sinclair name completed a half century of corporate life. These fifty years were marked by infant and adolescent perils, by crises in crude oil supply and finance, by defeats and triumphs. In sum, these years witnessed the adventurous life of one of the most interesting corporate citizens in American business history.   In its tenth year, Sinclair sales exceeded one billion gallons of refined products. In its thirty-second year, a half-billion-dollar annual gross operating income was reached. At age thirty-six, Sinclair joined the exclusive "Billion Dollar Club" of American industry, its assets employed in the business exceeding one billion dollars. Approaching the half century, Sinclair stockholders, 20,000 of whom had owned their investment for more than two decades, had an equity exceeding one billion dollars. And finally, a long-cherished ambition was attained: Sinclair's raw materials production from its own wells exceeded half of its refinery needs for the first time in the organization's modern history. At the half century, these milestones challenged Sinclair to consolidate its growth into greater profits in the years to come.   Here, in brief, is the story of those fifty years.

new crude oil research laboratory at Tulsa

in half a century,
Harry F. Sinclair's
flamboyant dream
becomes one of the
nation's large
industrial complexes

A frontier town named Independence was the spiritual birthplace of the billion dollar complex of companies known today as Sinclair. The pioneer challenge of free and open opportunity that motivated the founding of Independence, Kansas, also impelled one of its sons, Harry F. Sinclair, to create a resolute independent in the petroleum industry. The Sinclair companies were born of the indomitability—or, if you prefer, the plain Yankee cussedness—of a young man, not yet forty years old, who owned crude oil and refused to be told by his entrenched elders where to sell and at what price. One of the Sinclair companies makes its home in Independence, Kansas, to this day. So, too, does the Sinclair company spirit, which treasures its independent heritage and continues to pioneer.

Sinclair's pioneer independence, translated into imaginative enterprise, built the organization to a place among the giants of industry in less than half a century. Before its Fiftieth Birthday—May 1, 1966—bold management consolidated Sinclair's boisterous beginnings, and now thrusts aggressively forward into a confident future. Harry F. Sinclair envisioned in his first proposal back in 1916 an organization "engaged in all branches of the petroleum industry and international in its scope of operations." At the half century, with crude oil production on three continents and export sales to most of the world, Sinclair has achieved its stubborn founder's dream.

after half a century, Sinclair is:

among the top U.S. industrial corporations:

22nd in assets: $1,637,610,000□

22nd in invested capital: $1,030,484,000□

55th in net profit: $58,735,000■

46th in sales: $1,187,296,000■

▱ one of fewer than 60 U.S. corporations with more than a billion dollars of annual sales

▱ one of America's fast-growing per share equities for investors. The book value of Sinclair common stock has increased 265 percent since 1931

▱ one of a select group of New York Stock Exchange listed corporations with an unbroken dividend-paying record of more than a quarter century

□ *as of December 31, 1964*

■ *for the year 1964*

among the big 10 U.S. petroleum companies:

☐ seller of every 20th gallon of gasoline consumed in Sinclair's territory, a rate of 5,700 gallons every minute, day and night, around the calendar

☐ eighth in U.S. refining capacity

☐ largest direct deliverer of home heating fuel

☐ owner and operator of a pipe line system valued at $145 million, one of the world's largest and most efficient, which, with lines in which Sinclair owns partial interests, delivered one-ninth of all crude oil and petroleum products hauled by pipe lines in the United States

☐ supplier to 21,900 service stations and other retail outlets. 90 percent of the population in Sinclair's sales territory is within 75 miles of a Sinclair distribution point served by pipe line or water transport. This feature permits delivery to terminals with an economy and efficiency perhaps unmatched anywhere

☐ refiner of 4 percent of America's highest quality lubricants, serving many airlines and railroads, industries, space programs and national defense projects with more than 500 specialty oils

☐ owner or operator of tankers and barges on oceans, rivers and lakes as economical as any, under American registry, unsurpassed in technological advances and crew comfort

☐ a strategic leader in the development of petrochemicals, which have been called the "petroleum industry of the future." Sinclair is America's largest exporter of butadiene, and exports also more than 25 petrochemicals which contribute substantially to net profit

☐ for most of its fifty years a leading supplier of U.S. Navy fuel oils

champion:

As a champion of independent American business, Sinclair also is second to none. The organization has been for all its life a major factor in the survival of free competition in an area more essential to American life than any except food and shelter. Sinclair is a large purchaser of crude oil from independent operators in America. Its "Buy American" policy, sustained for fifty years, puts $400 million annually into the pockets of independent oil producers. Sinclair also sponsors and sustains about 26,000 so-called "little businessmen," who operate service stations, home fuel delivery systems, or local distributing centers, retailing Sinclair products.

in four
enormous industries

Sinclair, one of the largest independents to be organized in the oil industry since the trust-busting era, at age fifty exerts powerful force as an independent in four enormous industries: oil and gas production, manufacturing, transportation, and marketing. Thus the enterprise has made important contributions to keeping alive the independent American spirit throughout the national economy. Sinclair still emphasizes independence: for itself, its suppliers and dealers; and, for its customers, the right of free choice as an essential of American progress.

a new brand name

Sinclair added a new brand name, equated with superior quality, at a time when presumably all the big oil companies which the economy could support had been formed. Within six months of its founding, Sinclair went on to create enormous new wealth, investment and career opportunities, job security, vast tax revenues, and a dimension of independence in a vital industry, without all of which this nation would be measureably poorer.

At its Fiftieth Anniversary, Sinclair has made successfully the transition from thirty-three years of one-man leadership to a decentralized management team. In the process, the legacy of Harry F. Sinclair has been doubled, and the Sinclair complex of companies has become a billion dollar enterprise.

the next half-century

Sinclair faces its next half century in the turbulent population-exploding space age with confidence that its rate of growth—for a half century consistently exceeding the expansion of the national economy—would be sustained. But growth for bigness, the driving motive of Harry F. Sinclair, is now obsolete as an organizational life force. The accent of the new generation is on *growth for profit*.

Fifty Independent Years

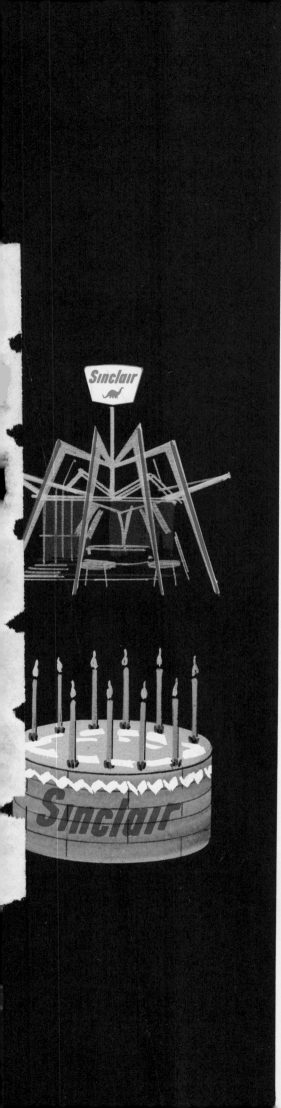

chapter 2:

success story:
Harry F. Sinclair's giant

Harry Ford Sinclair's father reared his younger son to be a small town druggist. But along with the pharmacy, the sire bequeathed his scion an overweening ambition, a gambler's courage, and an intuitive stubbornness perfectly suited to another destiny. Fate was scarcely subtle with young Harry Sinclair. It caused him to lose the drug store in a speculation at age twenty, just as an oil boom enveloped the community. Freed of his confining inheritance, penniless, product of the schools of frontier Kansas, Sinclair read correctly the juxtaposition of his stars and attributes, and headed for the oil fields. Thus began one of the great careers of the American petroleum industry.

First big crude oil discovery after organization of Sinclair enterprise was Garber Field, Oklahoma

Sinclair founded career on brashness and daring

Sinclair first sold lumber for oil derricks, buying and selling leases on the side. By train and buggy he ranged southeast Kansas and the Osage Indian territory now part of Oklahoma, sniffing likely drilling prospects, reselling for peanut profits. His zeal and "luck" attracted such moneymen as Chicago meat packer J. M. Cudahy and his field manager John F. Overfield, the Pittsburgh capitalist Theodore Barnsdall, and James F. O'Neill, president of the Prairie Oil Company.

investors with Sinclair amassed quick dividends

For his many sponsors, the young Sinclair organized small companies around single leases, with himself as salaried manager and usually treasurer; for his creative work he took a few shares of stock in each enterprise. When such leases yielded oil— as they did with uncanny frequency—the promoters sold quickly, reinvesting in new wildcat ventures flushed by Sinclair. The rich speculators needed a bird dog, and Harry Sinclair qualified; almost unfailingly he pointed lucrative ground. His managerial talents were also developing; no matter how small his investment was in any company, he insisted upon absolute control of its affairs, even though his salary for supervision was often a paltry $75 monthly. With control, he could buy and sell as opportunity offered momentary advantage in the precariously shifting fortunes of the oil fields.

The young druggist, Harry F. Sinclair, in 1896, on his mother's front porch

The older brother, Earl W. Sinclair, in 1893; he tempered Harry's enthusiasms

The drug store at 102 Main Street was briefly christened Sinclair & Company

A first triumph: handyman for others, Sinclair found oil at Wayside, Kansas

aggressiveness an attribute

Uncowed by his illustrious associates, he exhibited an extraordinary self-confidence which gave authority to his quick decisions. Still under thirty years old, he deferred to no one. An eastern magnate, director of one of Sinclair's little one-lease companies, described Sinclair's management to a friend: "He calls us together occasionally to tell us what he's done." The characteristics of his later life already were manifest. Said a colleague of him in retrospect: "He was shrewd but hearty, tough but genial, a masterful trader, a hard-driving sportsman. He was Mac-Gregor—where he sat, there was the head of the table."

Sinclair's diligent usefulness to others paid off in 1904. His drilling syndicate at Kiowa, Oklahoma, netted him $100,000. For the first time he had cash and—more important—the power to borrow. Quickly he developed the Canary field, Oklahoma, into 100 wells in 1905. The profit from this venture he cast into the Glenn Pool, Oklahoma's first huge producer. By 1907, he was the richest man in Kansas.

Following the oil play southwestward, Sinclair and one of his many partners, Patrick J. White, bought crude oil from wildcatters for ten cents a barrel (42 gallons) in every prolific field before pipe line outlets were available. Erecting steel tanks, the partners stored millions of gallons of bargain oil. When conditions stabilized, they sold the filled tanks at a $1.20 per barrel profit. By 1913 Sinclair bossed 62 oil companies, owned eight drilling rigs, and with his brother controlled a Tulsa bank. Producing from every mid-continent field, he settled in Tulsa, Oklahoma, as its first citizen.

First big strike: the Glenn Pool, Oklahoma, made Sinclair a millionaire

In new oil fields Sinclair capitalized on confusion, bought prolific leases from wildcatters for cash; here, Ranger (above) 1917; Seminole (below) 1923

Sinclair becomes largest oil independent in mid-continent

The year 1916 found Sinclair the mid-continent's largest oil independent. For himself and partners in various enterprises he sold 33,000 barrels of crude oil a day. But his individualistic temper was irked at the entrenched operators and their price policies. In one of his most famous snap judgments, Sinclair decided to fight the giants on their own ground. In one busy week he blueprinted a $50 million enterprise to be engaged in every branch of the petroleum industry: crude oil production, pipelining and other transport, refining, and world-wide marketing.

In the mid-continent, Cushing Field had spewed millions of barrels of oil in 1915 onto a market already oversupplied by the prolific Glenn Pool. The quoted price of $1.20 a barrel for crude was a fiction; the independents fought for life by sales as low as ten cents. Hundreds of oil leases and producing properties were for sale at the lowest prices in a decade, from 10 to 25 percent of their true value. Harry Sinclair knew the worth of each one; he began to take options.

automotive age begins

The historic era also favored bold enterprise in the petroleum industry. Europe was at war. Ocean vessels and navies, railroads and heavy industries, were converting from coal to oil fuel. The U.S. Navy alone estimated its fuel oil needs at nearly two million barrels a year, America's railroads at almost half a million barrels. There were 193 aviators, presaging the gasoline-powered invasion of the skies.

Continent-wide expansion was forecast, marked by construction of the coast-to-coast Lincoln Highway. Most significantly, Henry Ford's $350 Model T now rolled from a newfangled assembly line, and would increase the registration of U.S. passenger cars from 2,350,000 to 6,600,000 in a short three years, plus a total of 700,000 trucks, 158,000 farm tractors and 64,000 airplanes.

The era of the gasoline-burning internal combustion engine had begun, and with it the great expansion of the petroleum industry. Harry F. Sinclair could not have timed his new venture more propitiously.

By 1913 Sinclair ran 62 oil companies

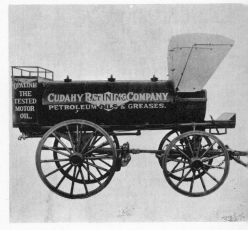

First Sinclair tank wagons were Cudahy resources

Sinclair and John Overfield, 1907. Even oil men preferred electric to gas buggy, but a year later Ford's Model T ignitioned auto age. Sinclair companies were built on service to gasoline-powered cars

TULSA DEMOCRAT / April 22, 1916

HARRY SINCLAIR HAS $50,000,000 PLANS FOR OIL CONCERN

Magnate Returns to Tulsa and Announces a Gigantic Corporation.

BUYS CUDAHY COMPANY'S HOLDINGS IN KANSAS

Many Refineries Through the Mid-Continent Field to Be Combined in Great Refining-Producing Organization.

Returning to Tulsa from New York this morning Harry F. Sinclair, muti-millionaire oil man, announced the formation of a $50,000,000 oil producing and refining company to operate in the mid-continent oil fields through Kansas and Oklahoma. The gigantic corporation will be the greatest organization of the kind perfected in recent years.

Mr. Sinclair was his usual reticent self when questioned regarding the plans for his project but declared that his plans have been perfected and that he already has taken possession of a large number of refineries, notably the holdings of the Cudahy Refining company with headquarters in Chicago and which has some of the most valuable holdings in the oil industry. One of the largest plants is located at Coffeyville, Kansas.

In his interview with a representative of the Democrat Mr. Sinclair d⸺

WE BEG TO ANNOUNCE

THAT THE NAME OF OUR COMPANY HAS BEEN CHANGED TO

SINCLAIR REFINING COMPANY

UNDER WHICH NAME

WE WILL CONTINUE TO CONDUCT OUR BUSINESS WITH THE SAME MANAGEMENT AND IN THE SAME MANNER AS IN THE PAST, BUT WITH LARGELY INCREASED FACILITIES.

WE THANK YOU FOR YOUR PAST PATRONAGE AND SOLICIT ITS CONTINUANCE.

THE CUDAHY REFINING COMPANY

PRESIDENT

CHICAGO, JANUARY 25TH, 1917

Key personnel for Sinclair came from Cudahy operation

Wall Street bankers finance oil combine for first time

Harry Sinclair's options consisted of 478 miles of gathering pipe lines to important fields, five refineries with a gross capacity of 15,300 barrels a day, the Cudahy marketing facilities in Kansas—and, more important, the Cudahy organizational know-how of experienced technologists and salesmen. Including his own resources, Sinclair controlled 532 wells capable of producing five and a half million barrels of crude oil a year. The package was valued at $50 million. With these assets Sinclair invaded Wall Street, which never had invested extensively in the new oil industry.

Eloquent Sinclair borrowed $20 million from New York bankers to buy assets then bargains due to the glut of mid-continent oil, and to fling a pipe line across the head of the mid-continent linking new refineries to be built at Kansas City and Chicago.

The Sinclair Oil & Refining Corporation was established on May 1, 1916. With characteristic daring and optimism, Harry Sinclair secured a charter "in perpetuity" from New York State. To shake off his provincialism, he established his headquarters in New York. Harry Sinclair himself still lacked three months of being forty years old. He and his company had joined the big powers of the oil industry.

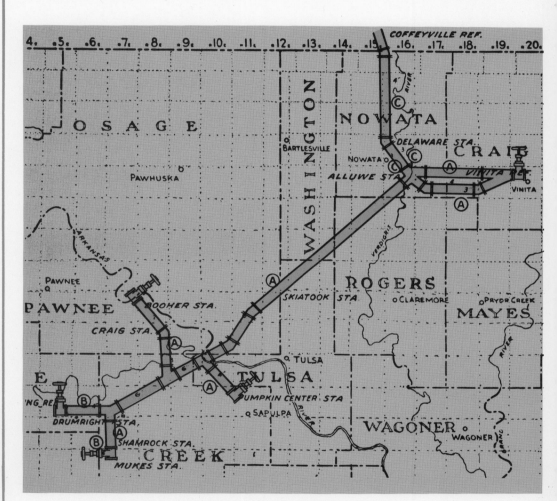

Sinclair's great pipe lines started here. The original 478 miles were a merger of three companies: Cudahy, Chanute and Milliken

The National Petroleum News

That Prints the News for The Independents

| Vol. VIII | CLEVELAND, OHIO, MAY, 1916 | No. 3 |

Biggest Independent Oil Deal Completed

Harry F. Sinclair's $50,000,000 Corporation Is In Operation; It May Take In Still More Properties

By A. V. Bourque, NEWS Correspondent at Tulsa, Okla.

young company assembled from odd bits and pieces in only one month's time

"The Sinclair Oil and Gas Company," said the National Petroleum News for May, 1916 of the operating subsidiary, "made oil history the past thirty days that has never been equalled or even approached in the history of the industry." In the brief space of a month, the Sinclair fledgling had soared to a height occupied by only nine other American petroleum companies.

What Harry Sinclair had done was to take advantage of industry conditions to assemble bits and pieces of depressed properties, five small but profitable refineries, and many untested production leases. But as an integrated operation it was more talk than fact. Whether the founder possessed managerial ability on a grand scale was unknown: he was a country boy who had never directed any enterprise which could not be tucked, along with sixty others, into a hip pocket. He had no organization, no technological skills, little administrative education. He needed specialized manpower at every level of a complex that was actually four huge businesses, each of which required special knowledge. His competition was sophisticated, entrenched and unsympathetic to his ambitions. Yet no publication predicted his failure, or even delineated the many weaknesses in both physical facilities and capital resources. With little except promises and options, his venture was a success.

Two factors greatly aided Sinclair to consolidate his blueprint. Huge over-production of oil forced many independent producers to sell their interests at a fraction of their true value. Sinclair's defiance of the established companies, which dominated the industry from production to sales, inspired many marginal operators to join and accept stock in the enterprise for their assets. Quickly Sinclair threw together a working concern.

Gaining refineries was most difficult. All of them were profitable, due to the automobile boom and World War I. Sinclair acquired five aging plants, three of which merely distilled the top fraction of crude oil into a gasoline. All were located in the oil fields rather than in rich markets. None challenged the big three seriously.

a management develops

One acquisition, however, was the Cudahy Refining Company, developed by the Chicago meat packer family. Its technological organization was exceptional, and it had retail distribution chiefly in Kansas. From Cudahy, Sinclair acquired the nucleus of a management which would lead the corporation for a generation. Cudahy was the keystone, for it brought in a refining genius in W. H. Isom and a sagacious director in Joseph M. Cudahy. To these, Harry Sinclair added an independent oil operator, A. E. Watts, his own assistant, W. L. Connelly, a pipe line engineer, John E. Manion, and as financial manager his brother Earl W. Sinclair. But the founder was monarch of his domain; his leadership was absolute, and would continue to be so for thirty-three years. The Cudahy sales organization gave Sinclair a famous trademark: Opaline, long a hallmark for superior lubricating oils and greases.

The refinery companies also owned 8,000 barrels of daily crude oil production. Sinclair controlled about 7,000 barrels himself, most of it in the south end of the Cushing Field. Together they balanced the 15,300-barrel daily needs of the primitive refineries.

Sinclair a shrewd buyer

But Harry Sinclair's plans were much more ambitious than anyone envisioned. With part of the cash from the $20 million financing acquired in New York, and as trades for corporate stock, Sinclair judiciously bought from among hundreds of bargains offered to him by hard-pressed independents. He added 8,000 barrels daily of crude oil in the proven Oklahoma fields of Healdton, Nowata, and the Osage Indian lands. Many of these buys continued to produce at the Fiftieth birthday. In midsummer he reached out northward to the new El Dorado field in Kansas, linking production there by pipe line to his refinery at Chanute. Also, he struck far southward, and again found a fabulous area: leases in the Damon Mound field in Brazoria County, on the Texas Gulf coast. These would yield 65 million barrels of crude oil during the next half century. On unproven land, the Company had forty rigs drilling wildcat wells.

First management, 1916, in Cushing field. Sinclair top row, fourth from left; to his right, Cudahy; fourth from right, A. E. Watts. This meeting approved midwest expansion with pipe line to refinery in Chicago

Then came a coup—his friends said it was typical Sinclair luck—which guaranteed success. A hundred miles west of Tulsa, a Sinclair wildcat penetrated a rich new oil basin with production at several depths. Sinclair had more than half the productive acreage under lease in this new Garber field. The oil was so rich that it sold for a premium price of $1.50 per barrel.

Now the founder invited his New York bankers to see the new oil empire. By special train he escorted what the Tulsa newspapers described as "the biggest concentration of capital in the history of Oklahoma." The gratified directors agreed to an ambitious expansion into one of the best retail markets in the world: the upper midwest.

Sinclair's first well in Texas, at Damon Mound on Gulf coast, in 1916. This rich find turned founder southward, inspired Sinclair Gulf Corporation

Garber field, discovered by Sinclair when company was only three months old. Huge production of $1.50-premium oils assured young enterprise's success, persuaded New York bankers to finance refineries at Chicago, Kansas City

bold enterprise challenges industry giants

Five months after the founding of Sinclair Oil & Refining Corporation, Harry F. Sinclair announced that he would build a new 8-inch pipe line from the Cushing Field in Oklahoma to East Chicago, with modern refineries at Kansas City and the Chicago ship channel. That he meant to battle the industry giants on their own ground excited the entire mid-continent. That the land acquired in East Chicago was within sight of Standard Oil's Whiting, Indiana, plant had defiant implications obvious to the trade. Exactly a month later, one thousand workers began to push the pipe line northward from Drumright, Oklahoma.

"We make everything," said an advertisement, "that can be made from petroleum." The sales book priced eighteen products: gasoline; a tractor distillate named Hi-podistal; kerosene; natural gas; bunker fuel for ships; tar, pitch, roof coating, turpentine, paint, leather preservative, medicinal mineral oil, and a half dozen oils and greases.

Sinclair now expanded its sales, heretofore confined to paltry outlets in Kansas. Before 1916 ended, the Sinco trademark adorned service stations from Oklahoma north to Iowa, from Denver east to Albany, N.Y. There was little rural business, since only 880,000 miles of U.S. road were even gravelled, and nowhere was there a continuous 50-mile stretch of pavement.

first year profits big

In its first 14 months, Sinclair produced six million barrels of crude oil worth $7.5 million. It sold 252 million gallons of products through wholesalers and 87 bulk plants, for revenues of almost $17 million and a net income of almost $9 million. Dividends paid equaled $5 a share, and assets employed in the business increased 40 percent. With some hyperbole, the president announced: "The corporation is better balanced, as to control of raw materials, pipe lines, refineries, tank cars, and distribution of refinery products, than any of its large competitors." In this statement, Sinclair roseately anticipated the completion of a dream; but he was on his way.

The instant success of the venture attracted eager investors. The first bond issue was convertible into common stock, a maneuver profitable at $55. When the common soared to $67, most of the bonds were converted; the company was free of this debt within a year. Harry Sinclair promptly promoted another $20 million bond issue with which to finance his new refineries and the pipe line.

The anticipated construction would make Sinclair the tenth largest oil company in America. Secure in his strength, Harry Sinclair proved the independence of his new enterprise. Throughout the mid-continent fields, others had always set the prices. On December 20, 1916, by now the purchaser of 20,000 barrels of crude oil a day, Sinclair posted a 10¢ per barrel price increase. The pricing control was broken.

Early Sinclair tank farm. Mid-continent prices changed 48 times, 1922-1927: from 20¢ to $1.50 per barrel. Company bought cheaply, then drew from storage when prices were high

SINCLAIR RAISES PRICE OF CRUDE OIL IN OKLAHOMA

Independent Concern Takes Lead in Fixing Quotation; New Valuation $1.30.

OPERATORS BELIEVE REAL FIGHT BREWING

New Organization May be Challenging Standard's Right to Control Field.

TULSA, Okla., Dec. 20.—(Special.)— The price of mid-continent crude oil was advanced to $1.30 by the Sinclair Oil and Gas company this morning.

Ten-Cent Advance.

This was a rise of 10 cents over the prevailing price of the past two days. This is the third time since the mid-continent field was opened that the price on the local market has been changed by any company except the Prairie Oil and Gas company or other corporations affiliated with the Standard Oil company.

Fight Brewing.

Independent producers here today proclaimed the bulletin issued by the Sinclair company as a break in the control which the Standard has experienced for many years over the mid-continent field.

Oil operators are inclined to believe the action of the Sinclair company will lead to a· fight between Sinclair and the Standard for domination of the Ok-

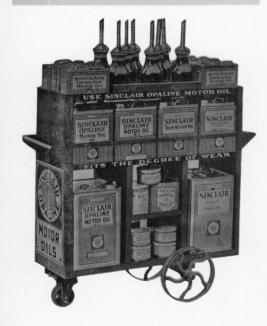

TULSA DEMOCRAT / Dec. 20, 1916

ADVANCE IN OIL TODAY IS THE FIRST GREAT VICTORY FOR INDEPENDENT OIL MEN

(By A. V. BOURQUE.)

At the opening of the market this morning, the Sinclair Oil & Gas Co. posted an advance of ten cents in the price of Mid-Continent crude, making the market at the time, $1.30.

There is a whole volume in the above statement. For it not only means that the producers of Oklahoma and Kansas are ten cents a barrel richer this morning than they were yesterday but, what is far more important, it means that, at least, the oil producers of the Mid-Continent field are out from under the domination of the Prairie Oil & Gas Co.

It has further significance. It also means that the day of the Prairie dictating the price in Oklahoma and Kansas has gone by. From a leadership that has lasted through might alone for many years, the Prairie has been overthrown by a company, less than nine months old and which is, today, the leading figure in the oil business of the Mid-Continent field.

Other Companies Are Silent.

The Prairie Oil & Gas Co. and the other purchasing concerns are silent regarding the action of the Sinclair organization.

The officials of the Prairie, Texas company and the Gulf in Tulsa refuse to make any statement, other than that they have not at this writing met the advance. They have referred the matter to their superior officers and are waiting on developments.

Their telephones have been ringing steadily ever since The Democrat made the news of the Sinclair advance known. But to all, they have said nothing and very little of that. They have been as silent as the grave.

The news of the catastrophe to the old pipe line companies traveled fast. And many were the predictions that they would meet the Sinclair advance before the day is over.

tle one-horse concern that posted the market. It is the largest independent company in America that took the decisive step. It is the second largest purchasing concern in Oklahoma and Kansas. It buys and has bought for some time, more oil than either the Gulf or the Texas company and by that we do not mean that it has only bought its own production. It is a real purchaser of oil and buys upwards of twenty thousand barrels daily from independent producers, in addition to what it produces. It has posted a price similar to the other companies. And it does its buying in a different way. The Gulf and the Texas company buy a large portion of their oil from their own concerns, which is merely a matter of bookkeeping. But the Sinclair Oil & Gas Co. pays cash for over 20,000 barrels of oil it buys in the Mid-Continent field from the independent producer.

The Sinclair company is in a position to buy oil and pay for it. And its action today will long be remembered, especially when it comes to a scramble between the purchasing companies for oil to keep their pipe lines and refineries busy.

The Sinclair-Cudahy Pipe Line company is rushing work on its line from the El Dorado field to the Chanute refinery. And work will soon be started on its main line to Whiting, Ind. And it will soon be as well equipped as any of the other big concerns in the way of trunk lines from the Mid-Continent field.

H. E. Sinclair is the most dominant figure in the oil business of America today. Always a leader in the history of Oklahoma and Kansas' oil business, his action this morning places him at the very head of the industry.

It was less than nine months ago that Mr. Sinclair launched the company which today leads all independent oil companies in this country.

epic pipe line completion makes Sinclair competitive with biggest in industry

As a small producer, fighting to move his crude oil from glutted fields to profitable markets, Sinclair had learned the value of ownership and control of pipe line transport. He had observed also that the movement of volatile products by railroad tank car was costly compared with the pipe line shipment of crude oil; obviously, refineries should be located near markets, not in the oil fields. All five of the Sinclair refineries were isolated.

In a $50-million operation, Sinclair made his embryo organization into an important petroleum complex. His new eight-inch diameter pipe line ran from the heart of the mid-continent oil fields to the heart of the midwest.

pipe line a 673-mile span

At East Chicago, Indiana, the terminus, and at Kansas City, Kansas, which tapped the populous Missouri and Mississippi valleys, refineries were built simultaneously with the pipe line construction, timed to go on stream when the crude oil supply reached them. The line was punctuated by twenty pumping stations. The pipe line alone cost $30 million; the balance bought refineries and marketing facilities. A crash program raced the pipe line to completion at the rate of a mile a day. On Lincoln's birthday, 1918, the job was completed. On Saint Patrick's day—a fitting time since most of the laborers were Irish—the line was connected to the refinery's first shell stills.

In the same month both new refineries began to spew gasoline and other products. Mr. Sinclair then announced that he was ready to supply all the petroleum needs of an area of middle America inhabited by 40 million persons.

The achievement impressed the United States government as well as Mr. Sinclair's investors and competitors. In recognition of his new eminence, Mr. Sinclair was appointed to the petroleum section of the World War I War Service Committee. His colleagues were the eleven most important oil men in America. They regulated the flow of America's petroleum resources to war purposes. The same dozen men became the nucleus which organized the American Petroleum Institute. Both Mr. Sinclair personally, and his boisterous, aggressive but precariously-financed business, had earned impressive prestige. A new giant was already established in the petroleum market place.

Heavy eight-inch threaded pipe was connected by hand. Huge wrenches, called tongs, weighed 500 pounds. Foreman rapped work rhythm on pipe with sledge

Rushing northward, crew laid 206 joints of eight-inch pipe in nine hour shift, after trenches were completed by steam-powered ditching machines

Dramatic race to build pipeline from Oklahoma oil fields to Chicago crossed Mississippi River at Fort Madison, Iowa, on ice in sub-zero weather. When ice melted, more than a mile of completed section sank snugly to river bottom

growth links mid-continent with entire upper mid-west

Completion of the pipe line gave Sinclair's refineries access to 90 percent of all the crude oil production in Kansas, Oklahoma and Texas. Now Sinclair could buy advantageously from independent producers anywhere in the mid-continent for delivery to its own refineries or—a profitable sideline—to those of its competitors. Along the line, 2 million barrels of storage capacity permitted the operating subsidiary to continue its policy of hoarding crude oil in depressed times for use when the price was high. The new line's capacity of seven million barrels a year could move one-sixth of all mid-continent crude oil production at that time.

private wire serves system

A by-product was the pipe line's telegraph system, used for dispatching; tied to Mr. Sinclair's New York office, it became a 2,700-mile private communications web that interlocked every operation from remote wells to sales offices.

An additional source of gasoline also was tapped to satisfy the voracious new auto industry. In oil fields such as Seminole and Cushing, Sinclair installed equipment to extract the "natural" gasoline from wet gas, then sold both gas and gasoline very profitably. The new refineries and natural gasoline plants combined to make the five original oil field refineries uneconomic.

Typical pumping station-bulk plant on new pipeline had storage (above) and pump house (below). Pumps were self-sufficient, burning crude oil from the pipeline

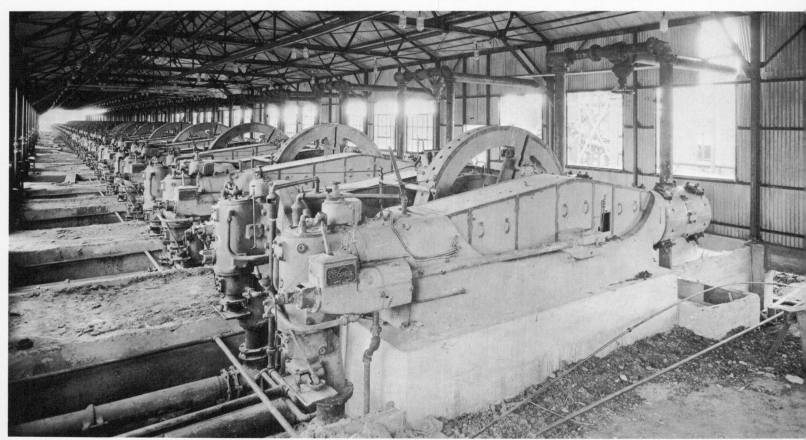

One of Sinclair's most profitable operations in early days was recovery of casinghead or "natural" gasoline from natural gas. Here, 32 four-cycle gas engine compressors were part of 62 employed in Seminole field, Oklahoma

accent on gasoline supply

The company's first refining experience proved the industry truism that a refinery is merely a huge experimental laboratory which is under constant improvement. Actually, the installations at East Chicago and Kansas City were outmoded soon after they went on stream for the first time.

First construction at the two new refineries consisted of shell stills which could produce 5,000 barrels daily of gasoline from the lightest fractions distilled off the top. After these shell stills were built, Sinclair's research chief E. W. Isom developed a thermal cracking method to produce more gasoline from crude oil.

Under Isom's new system, crude oil could be charged, fired, heated, pressurized and fractionated in a nearly continuous operation which yielded as high as 26 percent gasoline. Later, after improvements, the gasoline yield soared to 55 percent of the charge at a time when the industry average was much lower.

As Sinclair's gasoline output increased, each technological advance improved the quantity. The accent of the entire industry was on gasoline—all other petroleum products were subordinate. The race of producers to supply more and more gallons of fuel for the burgeoning auto industry had begun.

First construction at Sinclair's 290-acre plant in East Chicago. Note the proximity in background of Standard of Indiana's big Whiting, Indiana, refinery

First shell stills for running crude oil at East Chicago were built in 1917-1918. A year later first Isom stills (below) cracked oil by new process, increased quantity and quality, permitted extraction of more by-products

coal strike demonstrates superiority of oil fuel

Until the development of cracking processes, the East Chicago refinery produced twice as much fuel oil as it did gasoline. This lesser product glutted the market, the only outlet being the bunkering of lake vessels and a few railroad engines.

Harry F. Sinclair dramatically created a big new use for such fuels in the Chicago area in 1919. A coal handler's strike closed Chicago's public schools. On the advice of Sheldon Clark, a Sinclair vice president in Chicago, Mr. Sinclair sent a telegram to the Chicago mayor. "The welfare of the school children," he wired, "means more than the welfare of my corporation." He offered to convert all of Chicago's schools to oil heat without charge.

Under an enormous fanfare of national publicity, craftsmen from the East Chicago refinery designed, made and installed, in ten Chicago elementary schools, equipment converting their boilers from coal to oil, all in ten days' time. Clark turned the

Sinclair dramatized Chicago coal strike in 1919, converted 10 schools to oil burners, kept schools open. Three months later Sinclair's Chicago fuel oil business required 20 trucks

Until creation of products pipelines, Sinclair owned biggest tank car fleet in oil industry, 4,234 cars in 1920 and 6,071 by 1946, maintained big repair shops at Coffeyville, Kansas, paid $2,000,000 a month in freight charges

26

incident into a national demonstration of the superiority of oil heat. At the time, no commercial oilburners were available for industry, institutions or homes. But demand created a new industry. Before the end of the winter of 1919-1920, Sinclair's fuel oil business in the Chicago area required twenty big delivery trucks.

By now Sinclair had begun an assault upon the east coast, extending its marketing into New England by purchase of the Keith Oil Company, which owned service stations, and an ocean terminal at Tiverton, Rhode Island. The *Oil City Derrick*, a trade publication, commenting on this development, observed, "Probably no other company in all the history of oil has grown as rapidly in all the branches of the business as the Sinclair Oil & Refining Corporation has since it was organized less than two years ago."

personnel learn to handle highly volatile gasoline

With two new refineries on stream, the seven Sinclair manufacturing units produced, together with the "natural" gasoline plants, about 7,500 barrels of gasoline each day. The company now was required, without previous experience, to haul this volatile distillate all over mid-America, store it, and deliver it safely through crowded city streets. The technology of gasoline transport, however, was primitive.

Sinclair engineers and craftsmen solved by common sense the problems of high-speed, safe transfer of flammable liquids. Sinclair's shops designed and made hose connections, pumping systems, valves, nozzles and compartmented tanks. Truck manufacturers supplied a chassis, on which Sinclair mounted its own equipment. Safety procedures evolved by trial and error, each practical idea quickly permeating the system via the private telegraph or the personnel publication, *Sinclair Oils*.

From tank car, Tom Formby (above), distributed first Sinclair products in Trinidad, Colorado. Year later mules yielded to 1,070-gallon, three-compartment tank truck costing $4,745.95 plus $85 for lettering. Sinclair trucks were painted white from 1918 to 1920

Fleet of trucks rolling from East Chicago refinery to supply earliest Chicago service stations. These 3½-ton vehicles had special air springs on front axles

country boy philosophy spreads sale of products

Expansion of Sinclair's wholesale and retail outlets was largely what the salesmen, themselves midwesterners, called a "country boy operation." The bankers, less romantic, described it as shoestring financing. The company spent its own money for service stations only where "prestige" was important. Most of the pumps which gurgled Sinclair gasoline were operated by their owners who, like Mr. Sinclair himself, cherished their independence and individualism. There was no uniformity of station design or operation, no homogeneity of procedures. The attendants possessed the enthusiasm of men anxious to identify with the new auto supply industry which might make their fortunes.

No advertising was necessary. Until after World War I, gasoline demand outstripped supply, rising 38 percent between 1917 and 1919 to ten million gallons of gasoline a day.

Car owners greased, changed tires and tinkered their hobby vehicles as a fetish; no station offered such services. One grade of gasoline, one kind of crankcase oil, and one- and two-pound cans of grease were the service station's entire inventory.

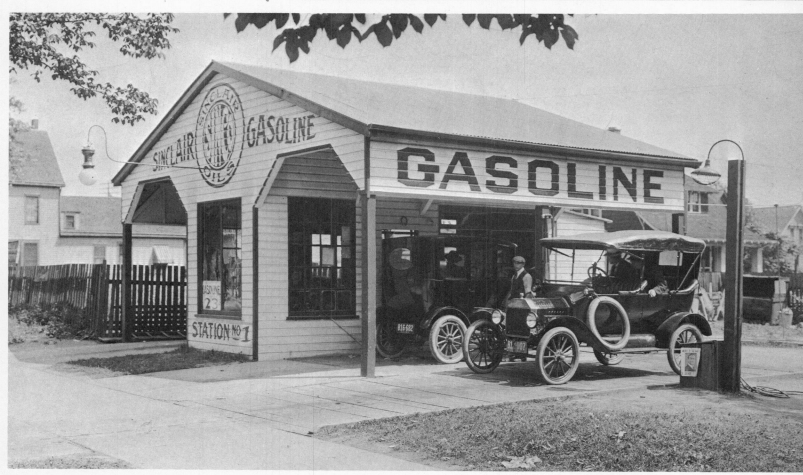

Two historic Sinclair service stations, each a pioneer in its area. At top, pentagon-shaped Chicago outlet at Ashland and Lawrence Avenues; below, in Buffalo, N.Y., at Fillmore and Peterson. Gasoline price 23¢, and no taxes

Self-employed commission agents built wholesale distributorships on shoestring; here, Wayne, Mich.

In Detroit, Sinclair absorbed company credited with city's earliest station, shown above, at Fort and First Streets. It sold gasoline, oil, No. 3 cup grease in cans, nothing else. By end of 1916, Sinclair served 19 outlets in downtown Detroit

In Cleveland, company division office occupied upper floors of first station

Thousands of independent dealers sold Sinclair products, served from nearest bulk plant. Sinclair salesmen's Ford runabouts were called "White Angels"

Sinclair was first big company to offer marina facilities to water craft. Here, three floating stations push up Erie Canal for duty in Chicago and Detroit, 1917. Sinclair is still a large Great Lakes supplier of such services

315,000-gallon daily flow of gasoline production spurs attention to sales

With almost frenzied speed, Sinclair and his colleagues built a system for wholesale and retail distribution and marketing, in anticipation of the enormous new capacities of the East Chicago and Kansas City refineries. Actually, neither of these units reached its rated capacity of 20,000 barrels daily until some years later, due to management insistence that the refineries produce no more than the organization could sell.

In its production policy, Sinclair was far ahead of the industry. Most producers and refiners belched out their daily capacities with no heed to the laws of supply and demand. Oversupply and over-production caused several severe oil industry depressions during years of general business prosperity. Mr. Sinclair, and both chief executives since the founder's day, have decried these wasteful gluts, and have advocated an orderly conservation and disposal of petroleum resources.

Even so, the relentless output of the refineries, operating on a continuous process around the clock, plus mounting reservoirs of gasoline extracted from gas, demanded the sale of huge quantities of products.

Press photo from Mexia, Texas, oil field, captioned "The Big Four," conceded Harry F. Sinclair's rise to top of industry. Others, left to right, A. E. Humphreys, Robert Stewart of Standard of Indiana, James O'Neill of Prairie

Early management kingpins included Director J. M. Cudahy, seated, and Sheldon Clark. Supersalesman Clark was also famous sportsman, a judge at "long count" Dempsey-Tunney fight, ended career chairman of Sinclair's directors

first year profits impressive

The pipe line in 1917 delivered seven million barrels of crude oil from the fields, a figure that increased to 12,500,000 barrels by 1920. The seven Sinclair refineries in 1918 poured forth a lush stream of 315,000 gallons of gasoline every 24 hours, the principal product made at the time. These had to be sold, and an organization had to be built from scratch, together with all the necessary facilities such as real estate, offices, plants and rolling stock. The two new refineries, utilizing modern techniques, added many products to the line: waxes, light and heavy fuel oils, exotic distillates, lubricants, paints. Markets had to be found for all of them.

In its first fourteen months Sinclair Oil & Refining Corporation earned $9.2 million and increased its assets by 40 percent to $70 million. By the end of 1918, the stated value of the corporation exceeded $110 million.

Even this was not enough for ambitious Harry F. Sinclair. He had already begun an expansion along the Gulf Coast which, in another year, would double the size of the organization, change its name, and launch it as an international enterprise.

Skilled personnel developed quickly as operations expanded; gauger measured oil depth by notched stick carried by buggy around tank farms

First uniforms for Sinclair service attendants, designed by Sheldon Clark in 1916, were introduced at opening of Chicago station on South Park Avenue

World War I diverted most male personnel from Sinclair stations in 1918, but "lady attendants" were not all as chic as these employed in Chicago

Company spirit evolved rapidly. Russell Burbridge, first Kansas City salesman, mounted oil drum on kerosene-lamped Model T. Barrel held tools, side curtains

denied expansion by his bankers, Sinclair builds big new company along Gulf and Atlantic coasts

Under booming war conditions, Harry F. Sinclair saw enticing opportunities to extend his oil domain along the Gulf of Mexico and the Atlantic coast. But his bankers refused to finance such expansion, since the $50-million building program was under way in the mid-continent. Sinclair's reaction was typical. He organized a separate complex in 1917 to fulfill his vision.

Sinclair Gulf Corporation was a wedding of three established enterprises, plus 16,000 barrels a day of oil production in Oklahoma, Texas, Louisiana and Arkansas, and a potential 150,000 barrels a day in Mexico. From a 15,000-barrel refinery at Mereaux, Louisiana, near New Orleans, 17 tankers spread products to ocean terminals as far away as New York harbor. A pipe line was under construction from Oklahoma to the Houston, Texas, ship channel, to serve a proposed lubricants refinery there.

Vital as were these acquisitions, an important extra was a staff of 4,000 employees skilled in key branches of the industry. Sinclair Gulf, at its birth, was almost as large as the other Sinclair corporation.

Early gusher at Smackover, Arkansas. Sinclair told bankers such purchases repaid buyer completely in two years

Sinclair Gulf merged several prosperous companies. Top, Mereaux, La., refined 4,700 barrels of Mexican crude daily into asphalt and road oils; middle, tank cars served 20-state market; below, one of the ships acquired

another big purchase

Simultaneously with creation of his new enterprise, Sinclair quietly bought control of facilities for an invasion of the east coast and Europe. In acquiring Union Petroleum Company, Sinclair sought only the concern's real estate at Marcus Hook, on the Delaware River near Philadelphia. This location, already a big tank farm and ocean terminal, was an ideal site for a Sinclair east coast refinery.

As usual with Sinclair's bargains, he gained much more than he sought. Union had Louisiana oil production with a small refinery at Westwego, an aged but important refinery at Wellsville, New York, four European sales offices, 400 railway tank cars, and an excellent management and operating personnel.

All these assets harmonized with a master plan for all his properties which Mr. Sinclair would reveal in September, 1919.

Union Petroleum brought Sinclair highest quality line of greases

Valuable skills came with Union. An early example of tank floated undamaged after dry construction

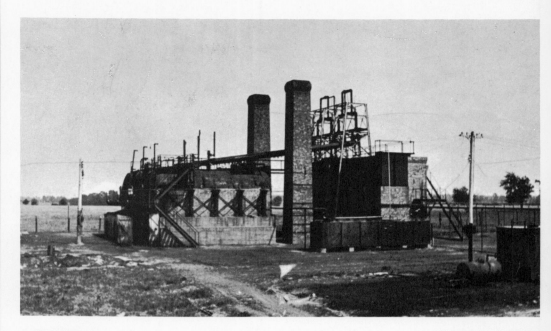

Union's Westwego stills (top) resembled Burton's, were modern for their day; from Wellsville (center) antiquated stills produced unsurpassed lubricating oils; Marcus Hook (below) in 1925, after first Sinclair construction there

Mexican crude oil leads to big business in Cuba

Mexican operations, Sinclair's first venture in foreign production, were good training for later explorations in South America and Africa. Everything was imported, from food to the 35,000 board feet of lumber in each derrick. All the technicians also were Americans. Most of the Mexican oil was almost as heavy as asphalt. Sinclair Gulf's potential was vast. Several wells on the 300 square miles of Mexican leases flowed 30,000 barrels a day. The fields were capable of 150,000 barrels daily without further development. In Mexico the problem was not to find oil, but to get it to market.

With American entry into World War I, all but two of Sinclair Gulf's tankers were preempted for war duty. The *Tamesi* and the *Panuco,* of 20,000 barrel capacity, cruised at only eight knots, too slow for convoy. Sinclair's bulk exports from Mexico were limited to the capacity of these vessels.

Actually, Sinclair Gulf did not need any imports at that time. The Houston refinery was unfinished. Ample crude oils were available in the prolific Healdton field of Oklahoma, augmented by a new discovery in Hominy, Oklahoma, where the oil was of such high grade that it brought a 25¢ per barrel price premium.

Sinclair's Walter Tschudin invented "Christmas tree" to curb high gas pressure

Lacking war-time steel, company had to produce into earth storage

Blowouts were frequent in Mexican drilling, crews were often soaked with oil

Cheap Mexican asphalt found ready market in huge U.S. road building program

34

sugar crop saved
by quick decision

Profitable use for the Mexican crude oil was found in 1918 when wartime food administrator Herbert Hoover sent a delegation to call one evening on Mr. Sinclair. The war had cut off Cuba's supply of coal; none was available to railroads or sugar refineries. The entire sugar crop appeared lost. In one of his memorable snap decisions, Sinclair, in one sentence, pledged to save the crop, then walked out on the astounded delegation, leaving details to his assistant, A. E. Watts. Within a month, technicians were converting the Cuban railroads and sugar centrals to oil fuel, and building tank farms. Soon the *Tamesi* and *Panuco* steamed in with raw, unrefined heavy Mexican crude to be burned directly without processing of any kind. Six million barrels of oil were delivered in the first year. Until the Castro regime, Sinclair was a major supplier of petroleum products in Cuba. Until 1938, when the Mexican government expropriated petroleum holdings, the oil for Cuba was supplied from Mexico.

Chiefly due to the Mexican production, Sinclair Gulf in 1918, its only full year as a separate corporation, produced 5,833,000 barrels of crude oil and earned a net profit of $2,245,000.

One of first "tankers" was Sinclair Gulf's Tamesi, converted cargo ship. Too slow for war duty, boat delivered Mexican crude to Cuba and Louisiana

The Badger, a Sinclair Gulf whale-backed barge, carried 8,000 barrels of oil from Tampico, then world's biggest oil port, to New Orleans and Cuba

Mexico: lifting cost in "light oil" wells consisted of turning a valve

Without pipe lines to oilfields, Panuco River was Sinclair lifeline; Mississippi steamboats were imported to push barges in shallow river

Houston refines lubricants, links Gulf and East Coast

Development of a refinery at Houston, Texas, was a far-sighted management operation. The object was two-fold: to build a lubricants plant; and to mount a terminal for the transport of cheap mid-continent crude oil, and finished products, by economical ocean transport to the American east coast. Neither of these goals was reached during the short life of Sinclair Gulf Corporation, but both were brought clearly into view.

By the time the first crude oil was run through the Houston refinery in January, 1920, Sinclair interests owned substantial production nearby in the Damon Mound and Columbia fields south of Houston, and a pipeline connection. During its first year, Houston averaged a throughput of 2700 barrels daily. Its first gasoline stills followed a year later.

Houston became vitally important to Sinclair operations at its inception. From the location on the ship channel, tankers soon delivered Sinclair products to distribution centers along the coast as far east as a terminal at Tiverton, Rhode Island, and crude oil to Marcus Hook, Pennsylvania. The Houston refinery also developed the famous H-C gasoline, Sinclair's first super-fuel marketed in 1926. The initials of this gasoline stood for "Houston Concentrate," but some advertising men preferred the term "High Compression."

Sinclair extended pipeline to new fields. Oklahoma spurs crossed Buffalo Creek westward (left) to Burkburnett, mucked eastward (right) to Hatfield, Ark. Transient towns such as Kiefer, Okla. (below) served line crews

War shortages of manpower and equipment forced Sinclair Gulf to extemporize in building Houston refinery Workers were hauled long distances in improvised trailers made in company shops; tractors were stripped trucks

Houston refinery was designed to produce high grade lubricating oil at first, not refined gasoline. From naphthenic-type crudes these shell stills took off lubricant cuts which were acid-treated to remove impurities, then filtered. Below, first 30-car train leaves new refinery in January, 1920, with high grade product

new domain is four times size of former corporation with international markets

In September, 1919, Harry F. Sinclair gathered all of his manifold petroleum operations together. He created the Sinclair Consolidated Oil Corporation, a holding company for 28 operating subsidiaries. From the outset, the group was important in the oil world, a truly integrated structure through which flowed every process of the industry from crude oil production to marketing, both at home and abroad.

The Sinclair domain now was four times the size of the original company. But its stated assets of $216 million were optimistic. A realistic write-down in 1932 reduced the computed book value of stock from $43.77 to $18.36 a share, even though by then assets had doubled.

After the consolidation, the new organization had 1,761 oil wells in the United States and Mexico, producing 40,000 barrels of crude oil every day. From ten refineries gushed 1,260,000 gallons daily. Seven extraction plants made 22,000 gallons daily of "natural" gasoline from 66 gas wells. The pipe line was the second-largest U.S. system, serving 90 percent of mid-America. Shipping totalling 154,000 tons carried Sinclair wares along the coast to strategic terminals from Houston, Texas, to New York harbor and on to Tiverton, Rhode Island. Ninety percent of the Mexican oil was sold in Cuba, while 85 percent of the lubricating oils and greases from Wellsville—unsurpassed in quality—were distributed in Europe. Intensive retail sales had been established in 20 states. Of the nation's gasoline outlets, Sinclair owned 400 and served 800 others. It was a leading supplier in the rapidly expanding fuel oil market, and one of the largest exporters of petroleum products in bulk.

All this yielded, in the first full year, net earnings of more than $18.5 million. But more than that, it made Sinclair a front runner in the race for service to the incredibly-proliferating automotive industry. In 1919, there were more than six million pleasure cars in America. By 1929 there would be that many new registrations each year. The Sinclair companies now set out to get and hold the petroleum products bonanza generated by the internal combustion engine boom on the road, at sea, in the air, in industry and on the farm.

SINCLAIR CONSOLIDATED STOCK HAS BEEN LISTED

TOTAL ASSETS ON JUNE 30 WERE $216,763,156, CURRENT ASSETS $34,721,435 AND CURRENT LIABILITIES $27,019,859

Sinclair Owns and Leases on 520,000 Acres Here and in Canda, 152,500 in Mexico, 10 Refineries and Marketing Stations in This Country, Mexico, Central and South America, Cuba and Europe

New York Stock Exchange has acted favorably on the application of the Sinclair Consolidated Oil Corporation and listed 2,887,982½ shares of capital stock, without nominal or par value, with authority to add 2,612,017½ shares, making the total amount to be listed 5,500,00 shares.

Sinclair Consolidated as of June 30, 1919, bad assets totaling $216,763,156. Capital assets including real estate, oil and gas leases, oil wells, equipment, etc., are given as $178,724,002. Current assets amounted to $34,721,435 and current liabilities $27,019,859.

Through its principal subsidiaries—Sinclair Oil & Refining, Sinclair Gulf and Sinclair Consolidated Oil, the new company owns oil and gas leases on approximately 520,000 acres in practically all of the known oil fields in Kansas, Oklahoma, Texas, Louisiana, Kentucky, Tennessee and Canada. About 30,000 acres are producing, the balance being undeveloped.. Through Mexican subsidiaries Sinclair owns oil and gas leases on approximately 152,500 acres of land scattered through the known oil fields in both heavy and light oil districts. Thus far drilling has been done only on 5,200 acres of this Mexican land.

Sinclair's subsidiaries of June 30 last had 1,763 oil wells, 66 gas wells and 135 drilling wells, producing about 40,000 barrels daily. But potential production is greatly in excess of this figure. It is estimated that one Mexican well alone is capable of producing more than 75,000 barrels daily.

Through other subsidiaries, Sinclair has a concession to exploit 988,416 acres of land in Costa Rica and 1,280,000 in Panama. Wells are now being drilled on land covered by these concessions.

Sinclair owns 4,024 tank cars, 11,000 acres of coal land in Illinois; ten refineries with an approximate daily capacity of 50,000 barrels, located at East Chicago, Ind., Kansas City, Chanute and Coffeyville, Kans.; Vinita, Muskogee and Cushing, Okla.; Houston, Texas, New Orleans, La., and Wellsville, N. Y., and approximtely 2,443 miles of trunk and gathering lines in Texas, Oklahoma, Missouri, Kansas, Illinois and Indiana. The main trunk extends from the Ranger field, Texas, to East Chicago Ind.

Sinclair also owns 10,000 tanks in the various oil fields with a capacity of more than 15,000,000 barrels. The average monthly storage is 5,000,000 barrels.

For the purpose of maintaining its foreign commerce, Sinclair owns and operates 5 ocean-going tank ships, 2 ocean-going barges, 5 tugs, and operates additional ocean-going ships. Supplementing this equipment Sinclair also has a considerable river and harbor fleet. The corporation's seven gasoline plants manufacture approximately 30,000 gallons daily.

For the distribution of its crude oil and manufactured products Sinclair has marketing stations throughout the United States, Cuba, Central and South America, Mexico and Europe.

Neither the corporation or any of its subsidiaries has outstanding any preferred stock or bonded debt except $2,750,000 7% pipe line bonds, $884,560 Sinclair Oil & Refining Co. equipment trust notes, $635,910 Sinclair Refining Co. equipment trust notes, $185,395 Sinclair Gulf notes, $93,850 Union Petroleum Co. sundry mortgages, $61,493 Freeport & Mexican Fuel Oil Co. equipment trust notes, $22,500 Freeport & Tampico Fuel Oil Co. purchase money obligations, and a $1,600,000 mortgage on Sinclair's Liberty tower building

Income account of Sinclair Oil & Refining Corporation and subsidiary companies for the six months ended June 30, 1919 compares with the six months ended December 31, 1918 and the year ended June 30, 1918, as follows:

	6 mos ended June 30,'19	6 mos ended Dec. 31,'19	Year ended June 30,'18
Net earnings	$7,408,421	$8,501,655	$11,854,734
Miscellaneous income	121,096	24,291	80,111
Total income	$7,529,517	$8,525,946	$11,934,845
Int, Fed taxes, etc..	*1,066,495	1,327,338	2,601,495
Depr, depl, amortiza	*......	5,029,987	4,669,874
Net income	$6,463,022	$2,168,621	$4,663,476

Liberty Tower in financial district bought for new global headquarters

Scene in Mexico: drilling site and accommodations camp

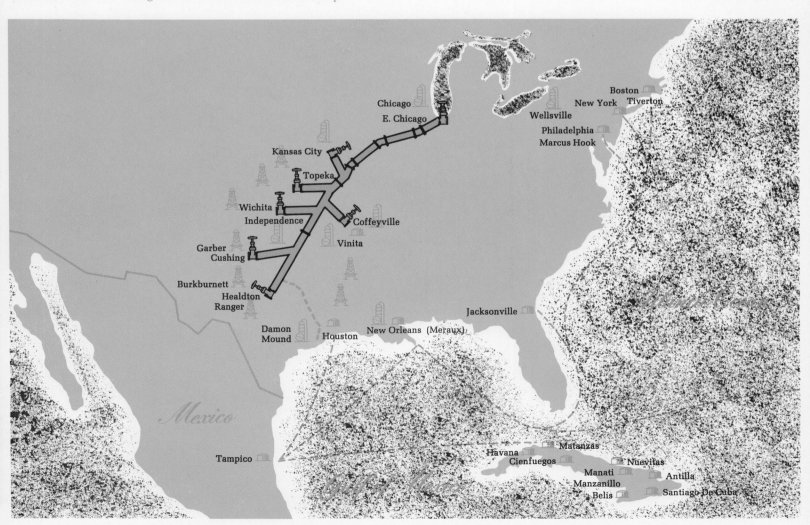

System after the consolidation. In 1923, the pipe line (dotted) was extended to link Gulf with Great Lakes

powerful fuel, rugged oil demonstrated by racing champions

Word of mouth praise, free publicity, and accessibility were the foundations of Sinclair's program to entrench its position. The public made no distinction between the products of companies; it bought what was handiest.

With effective distribution under the Sinclair brand in less than one-half of the nation, the retail marketers rejected national advertising. Promotion aimed to prove that Sinclair fuels had more power, Sinclair lubricants more stamina, than those of competitors. Further, an entirely new concept was developed: that service to car owners was of major importance, since the public knew almost nothing about the mechanics and maintenance of automobiles.

The power and durability superiority of Sinclair products were demonstrated by champions of the new sports craze—racing of internal combustion vehicles. Tailored white Palm Beach coveralls proclaiming the Sinclair name were worn by many speedsters of the 1920s: Gar Wood, supreme on the water; Floyd Clymer, the fastest motorcyclist; road and track auto winners Tommy Milton, Ralph DePalma, Gaston Chevrolet, Cannonball Baker and Art Kline. The publicity of their exploits enhanced Sinclair's stature, so that independent service station owners solicited Sinclair franchises. Thus were gained greater concentration of sales in its market areas, reduced costs, and widened coverage.

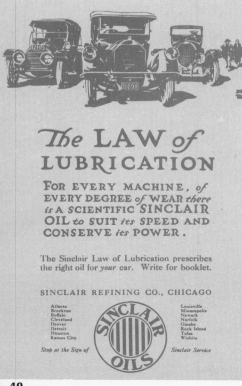

Intense program to prove superior power and lubricants to farmers paid off when Sinclair secured more of this market than did any other single supplier

Many speed racers of 1920's used Sinclair products. Here is Tommy Milton's fastest car on earth after traveling 156 miles per hour at Daytona Beach

At Indianapolis in 1920, Sinclair's tent was so popular that its gasoline was expended during trials, none remaining for main Memorial Day event

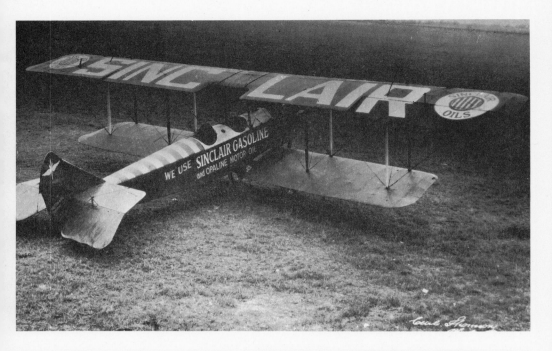

Sinclair supplied new air industry, set up service units on cow pasture airports as 64,000 aviators. 100 air companies emerged from World War I

Two of Gar Wood's famous Miss Americas, fueled exclusively by Sinclair, first speedboats to attain 75 miles an hour, won all major aquatic events

Gar Wood first lifted Harmsworth Trophy from British at Cowes Regatta in 1920

sales hit billion gallons on offers of service plus aviation-grade fuels

Technological service to car owners began in 1920 with publication of Sinclair's *Law of Lubrication*—a new scientific program to reduce engine wear. At the time the public was offered 160 brands of automobiles, 240 kinds of trucks, 150 different farm and industrial tractors. These varied widely in maintenance requirements and quality, but owners made no distinction in servicing them. Sinclair was a leader in educating drivers in vehicle care.

The next step was the modern service station, also pioneered by Sinclair. The first one opened in Chicago in 1922, taking maintenance out of the do-it-yourself class in back alleys. Now filling stations offered oil change, greasing, tire repairs, wash jobs, free air, minor mechanical repairs, and a profitable sideline in tires, batteries and accessories, which in the trade have been called TBA ever since. The automobile tourist was also a phenomenon for him, Sinclair's super-stations installed rest rooms.

The big money was in gasoline. The oil companies competed fiercely and expensively for that business. To cut costs, Sinclair refineries installed stills which "cracked" gas oil to yield double the amount of gasoline, fewer hard-to-sell by-products. This in turn put pressure on distributors to market the higher volume—an endless round robin. Sinclair's refining capacity jumped from 45,000 barrels a day in 1920 to 100,000 barrels in 1926 to 150,000 barrels in 1932. The cost for refinery construction in this expansion was more than $87 million.

First expert lubrication pioneered by Sinclair "Greasing Palace" 1922

Earliest modern service station was Sinclair's "Greasing Palace" in Chicago, catered to women by advertising cleanliness, offered rest rooms to tourists

Iowa (upper) and Missouri stations sold 40,000 gallons yearly in 1920s

Accent on service caused such innovations by Sinclair as windshield wiping, interior vacuum cleaning, springs oiling, and bearing greasing

first super fuel spurs sales

In 1926 Sinclair leaped ahead of most of its competitors with H-C, the industry's original high octane premium gasoline for motor cars. The octane race exploded on the industry in 1924 with general distribution of ethyl, an anti-knock additive. Unable to secure the ethyl franchise, Sinclair produced a 72-octane auto fuel, better than anything then marketed. Lindbergh's flight to Paris the following year was on 73-octane gasoline. H-C sold at a premium of only two cents, while ethyl added to regular gasoline cost from four to seven cents extra per gallon.

With H-C, Sinclair's sales crossed the billion gallon mark in 1926. Gasoline alone totalled 683 million gallons sold, up 10 percent in one year. This was the third largest gallonage among American companies, six percent of the total market. Of this, three-fifths were sold by Sinclair's own service stations or its dealers.

First cracking stills at Houston (above) and Marcus Hook (below) extracted more gasoline from crude oil, reduced percentage of hard-to-sell by-products

New England sales invasion speeded by tanker terminal at Tiverton, R.I.

These thermal cracking stills at Marcus Hook, built in 1931, replaced original 1925 stills

during depression years canny sale, purchases double Sinclair in size

The automotive boom of the 1920s caused such competition in the petroleum industry that gasoline prices were steadily eroded. At retail, the pre-tax price per gallon shrivelled from 25 cents in 1918 to 16 cents in 1930. As the great economic depression closed in, many heretofore blue chip oil companies, drained by a decade of expensive expansion amid price cuts, faced ruin.

Sinclair was in no better financial shape than its competitors. From 1920 to 1925 the Sinclair companies earned a net profit of $28,998,000, but only $4,895,000 was retained in the business. The balance of $24,103,000 was distributed as dividends. Thus most of the enormous physical expansion of this period was financed by borrowed capital.

As early as 1927 Mr. Sinclair had begun to compile a scrapbook which stalked two important rivals. They were the giant Prairie, a Rockefeller interest as big as Sinclair Consolidated, and a Wyoming enterprise, Producers and Refiners Corporation. Just as the depression began, the new Ajax pipe line through the mid-continent siphoned off most of Prairie Pipe Line's traffic, jeopardizing the entire Prairie system. Harry F. Sinclair, who had foreseen this, made the boldest gamble of his life.

During the recession year of 1921, a half interest in the pipe line subsidiary had been sold to Standard Oil Company (Indiana). As the depression of 1930 deepened, Mr. Sinclair sold to the same rival, for $72.5 million cash, the remaining half interest in the pipe line company, along with its 50-percent interest in the Sinclair Crude Oil Purchasing Company. The industry said he had committed suicide. Instead, he saved his company's life. Securing another $33,500,000 through the sale of a new common stock issue, Sinclair retired pressing bank notes. He then braced for the economic depression with cash in hand, ready to buy distressed companies which would dovetail handily into the Sinclair system.

First to fall was Pierce Petroleum Corporation, originally part of the Standard Oil Trust, an important retailer in the southern states. This deal cost no cash, only stock. For the first time in its history, Sinclair that year sold a billion gallons of gasoline.

Prairie joins Sinclair

Then in 1932 Sinclair annexed the assets of the Prairie pipe line and producing companies for stock valued at $136 million. This acquisition gave Sinclair the largest pipe line system in America, 36,000 barrels a day of oil production, many other assets, and immense prestige. The Sinclair complex suddenly had doubled in size.

A few months later, again in an exchange of stock, Sinclair acquired the Rio Grande Oil Company, which produced crude oil and marketed in California. Now Sinclair had reached the West coast.

During all these events, the holding company lost the Sinclair name, and became simply Consolidated Oil Corporation, a title which continued until the modern name Sinclair Oil Corporation was assumed in 1943. A realistic write-down of $143 million in assets still left Consolidated in 1933 the eighth largest oil company in America. It resumed in 1934 quarterly dividend payments which have continued uninterruptedly since.

TULSA WORLD / April 7, 1932

PRAIRIE SINCLAIR MERGER RATIFIED

Consolidated Corporation Takes Place Among Oil Giants

SETTLED BY VOTE OF 88.17 PER CENT

Objections of Small But Militant Minority Overridden

By PAUL HEDRICK
Oil Editor The World

INDEPENDENCE, Kan., March 1.—The Consolidated Oil corporation of New York, the newest of American oil giants, came into existence today as a result of a flood of votes at three company meetings, two here, and one in New York City.

Stockholders of the Prairie Oil and Gas company this morning, and the Sinclair Consolidated Oil corporation at noon, and the Prairie Pipe Line company this afternoon voted almost unanimously to consolidate ther assets and properties and create a new oil unit.

Objections by a small but militant minority, which had sought to en-

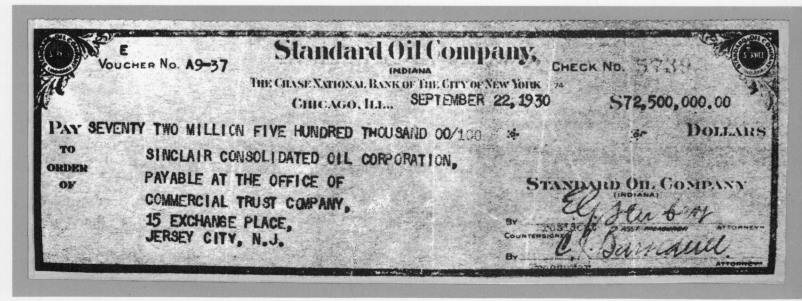

Teapot Dome controversy involves Sinclair indirectly

During the decade of the 1920s, the Sinclair organization became involved in the Teapot Dome controversy. A contract to develop naval oil reserve lands in Wyoming was awarded in 1922 to Mammoth Oil Company, a structure organized by Mr. Sinclair to operate in Teapot Dome. Sinclair Consolidated Oil Corporation, as the holding company was known then, traded 250,000 of its common shares for a 25 percent interest in Mammoth, with an option on sufficient additional stock to assure ultimate control. In 1924, Sinclair Pipe Line Company (50 percent owned by Sinclair Consolidated Oil Corporation) extended its system 700 miles to Wyoming, at a cost of about $21 million. Under Mammoth's obligation to the government, oil terminal facilities were constructed at the Portsmouth, N.H., Navy Yard costing $1,340,000.

Alleging fraud in the award of the Teapot Dome contract, the government sued in 1924 to cancel the arrangement with Mammoth. The trial court held the lease legal and dismissed the complaint; but in 1927 the U.S. Supreme Court, on appeal, voided the contract on technical grounds, though finding "no direct evidence of fraud." A jury which deliberated only forty minutes acquitted Mr. Sinclair of a criminal charge of conspiracy to defraud. The use by Mr. Sinclair of private detectives to keep the jury under observation during the trial drew a sentence for contempt of court. During the long controversy, Mr. Sinclair gave 175,000 words of testimony before twelve legislative committees, disdaining the fifth amendment; but for refusing to answer one question which his counsel considered not to be pertinent to the legislative inquiry, Mr. Sinclair was held to be in contempt of the Senate. On the contempt citations, he spent six and one half months in the Washington, D.C. House of Detention in 1929.

Both Mr. Sinclair and Mammoth Oil Company lost heavily in the Teapot Dome venture, the naval reserves being unprofitable. In 1928, Mr. Sinclair voluntarily returned to Sinclair Consolidated the 250,000 shares it had invested in Mammoth, plus $400,000 paid in dividends. During the entire seven years of the Teapot Dome-Mammoth Oil Company dispute, Mr. Sinclair continued as chairman and chief executive officer of Sinclair Consolidated, with the unanimous support of his directors, who tendered him a public vote of confidence as he left New York to serve his sentence.

Pierce purchase included two roadside hotels in Ozarks, forerunners of motels; Sinclair's sales crews (above) sold big gallonage in southwest states

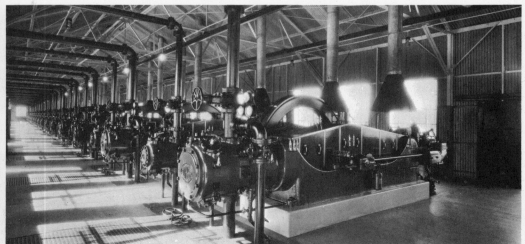

Prairie acquisition brought 6,400 oil wells (some shown above with natural gasoline plant), and excellent equipment such as this compressor room

bankrupt companies saved by Sinclair's management during depression years

Expansion of the Sinclair enterprise during the depression years 1930-1936 was partly due to the salvage of companies in receivership or bankruptcy. Except for Sinclair participation, they would have disappeared, at huge loss of jobs, investments and community prosperity. One such company was Producers & Refiners Corporation.

This oil company operated chiefly in Wyoming, Idaho and Utah, with some oil production, many untested but promising leases, large but undeveloped natural gas reserves in Wyoming and the Texas panhandle, and an 8,000-barrel refinery in the company-owned town of Parco, Wyoming. More than 600 families relied on Producers and Refiners, or Parco as it was called, for their livelihood. When Sinclair took over the Prairie companies, it inherited 65 percent of Parco. This was a dubious asset. Prairie had loaned Parco more than three million dollars and had guaranteed $10 million of Parco's debts. One month after the Prairie merger, Parco defaulted its notes. Sinclair had to pay them.

Parco went into receivership. At court-ordered public auctions in 1934, Sinclair bid in most of the Producers and Refiners properties, paying for them with about $10 million of its $13,600,000 accrued claims against the company. Developed soundly by Sinclair management, the former Parco facilities became assets to their communities, and keystones of Sinclair operations in the Rocky Mountain region.

Parco purchases increased gasoline recovery from gas through plant at Bairoil, Wyoming; also for first time gave Sinclair important natural gas cash crops

Producers and Refiners acquisition brought company an 8,000-barrel refinery, complete town, tourist hotel, at Parco, Wyoming, plus Mountain States sales

NEW YORK SUN / March 25, 1937

The Investor's Column

Richfield Oil Subscriptions Leave No Securities to Be Underwritten.

Subscriptions to the securities issued by the reorganized Richfield Oil Company of California are reported to have exceeded right issued, with the result that no securities will be available to the underwriters.

The sale of the new securities completes a reorganization task on which creditors of the bankrupt company had been working for several years. The Richfield Oil Company passed into the hands of receivers in 1931.

During that period several bids for the properties were put in by both the Standard Oil Company of California and the Consolidated Oil Cor-

poration. Now, the properties have virtually passed under the control of the Sinclair group, associated with the Cities Service Company, the Richfield Oil Company's largest creditors

A number of involved and troublesome questions, which hampered efforts to reorganize the Richfield company, had to be adjusted before the plan could be formulated and pu

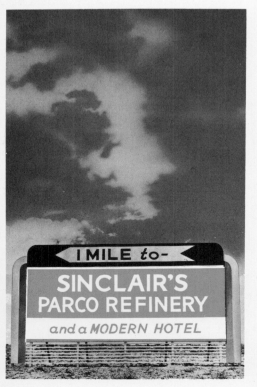

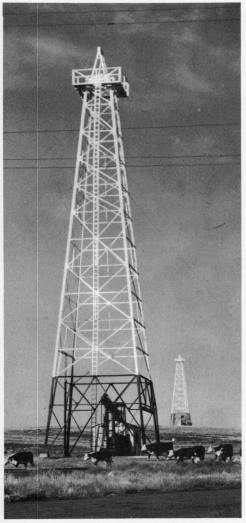

Wyoming reached million barrel yield in 1938; above, Lost Soldier field

Pennant, colored green, was cut-rate competitor in depression price wars

Richfield also salvaged

An even larger salvage operation was the rescue in 1936 of Richfield Oil Company of California, a depression victim. For several years, Richfield was operated by a Federal Court-appointed receiver. Sinclair helped the receiver by purchasing Richfield's East coast marketing subsidiary. Richfield's remaining assets were offered for sale by court order in 1936, but no buyer would pay the court-fixed upset price. Subsequently, Sinclair participated in a plan of reorganization under the Bankruptcy Act which resulted in a new entity, Richfield Oil Corporation. To the new structure were transferred the properties of Rio Grande Oil Company, in which Sinclair then owned a 50 percent interest. Sinclair also contributed many key employees, its operating skills, and a refinery management agreement. Under the court-approved reorganization, Mr. Harry F. Sinclair became a director and Chairman of the Board.

Richfield merged with Atlantic Refining

On December 30, 1965, stockholders of Richfield Oil Corporation and The Atlantic Refining Company approved a merger of the two firms, as of January 3, 1966.

Sinclair Delaware Corporation, a wholly-owned subsidiary of Sinclair Oil Corporation, owned 2,447,162 shares of Richfield common stock and $15,294,700 face value of Richfield Convertible Debentures at the time of the merger.

Sinclair received 2,447,162 shares of a new $3.00 Cumulative Convertible Preference Stock of The Atlantic Refining Company. The debentures are now convertible into 436,991 shares of said Preference Stock. On date of merger said securities had a market value of around $220 million.

DENVER POST / *April 17, 1934*

CHICAGO JOURNAL OF COMMERCE / *Feb. 2, 1932*

RICHFIELD OIL REORGANIZING AT LAST SURE

$15,500,000 to $20,000,000 New Money Expected to Bolster Working Capital

SAN FRANCISCO, Feb. 19. — (Special)—Six years' efforts to get the Richfield Oil Company of California out of receivership promised to be crowned with success today when the last opponents of the reorganization plan of August 20, 1936, acceded to the majority view. Subscription certificates, from the sale of which it is hoped to raise between $15,500,000 and $20,000,000 to bolster working capital of the new company, will be made available to security holders tomorrow.

What appeared to be the last obstacle was removed when Federal Judge William P. James granted a motion by Roy P. Dolley, representing dissenting creditors of Richfield and Pan American Petroleum Company, to dismiss a motion to vacate the court's order with reference to distribution of subscription rights.

"Adjustment Is Satsifactory"

"We now move for a dismissal of the motion," Mr. Dolley's plea stated,

CONSOLIDATED PLANS INTENSIVE SALES DRIVE IN MOUNTAIN AREA

Acquisition of Parco Properties Gives Sinclair Interests Favorable Position—Distribution System Already Established.

The Consolidated Oil corporation, a 100-million-dollar Sinclair holding company, is going to make an intensive drive for the gasoline and oil business of the Rocky Mountain district.

W. L. Connelly, chairman of the board of directors of the Sinclair-Prairie Oil company, said so Saturday as he passed thru Den-

at twentieth birthday companies consolidate big operational gains

The Sinclair companies emerged from the 1930-1935 depression with huge gains in every operation, and with the holding company now transiently known as Consolidated Oil Corporation.

During the six critical years, the operating units had stepped up crude oil production by 75 percent, refinery runs by 51 percent. Marketing flourished in most states, Cuba, Mexico and Europe. Gasoline sales of 1¼ billion gallons—up 30 percent—were matched by balancing disposal of subsidiary products including, for the first time, important quantities of natural gas. Internal research had developed items which had won an impressive share of the nation's industrial lubricant business, and for a twentieth anniversary gift impelled Sinclair forward with Tenol, a pioneer diesel lubricant. The two-decade anniversary year gross income was $215 million and the net $16,728,000.

The mere logistics of serving Sinclair's markets required 14,000 miles of pipe lines, 6,446 railroad tank cars, 100,000 tons of ocean tankers, nine deep water terminals, 2,170 bulk plants, 8,100 service stations which were company-owned or held under long-term lease, 21,000 other retail outlets, and 20,000 employees. In twenty years Sinclair had achieved its original goal: to become big. This achievement was followed by another cycle of frenzied growth and then—world war.

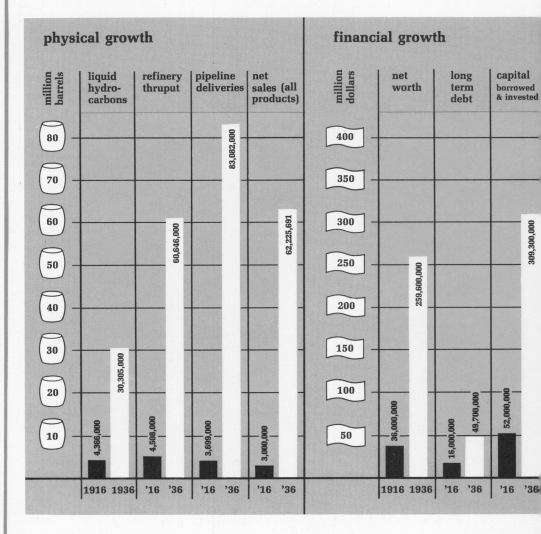

physical growth

million barrels	liquid hydro-carbons	refinery thruput	pipeline deliveries	net sales (all products)
80			83,082,000	
70				
60		60,646,000		62,225,691
50				
40				
30	30,305,000			
20				
10				
	4,366,000	4,508,000	3,699,000	3,000,000
	1916 1936	'16 '36	'16 '36	'16 '36

financial growth

million dollars	net worth	long term debt	capital borrowed & invested
400			
350			
300			300,000,000
250	259,600,000		
200			
150			
100			
50		49,700,000	52,000,000
	36,000,000	16,000,000	
	1916 1936	'16 '36	'16 '36

Wellsville largest refinery using only Pennsylvania grade crudes

Offshore wells at Nueces Bay, Texas prove oil discovery more difficult

48

Highly successful research extends sales line to two hundred products

Wellsville exports 85 percent of its lubricants to Europe

With unexcelled quality lubricants, first tamper-proof can introduced

THE WALL STREET JOURNAL / June 5, 1936

Consolidated Oil Corp. Acquired Many Properties in Last 5 Years

Crude Production Increased 76%

Gasoline Sales Gained 30% in Period, With Runs to Stills Up 51% 12 Refineries in Operation

The acquisitions of additional subsidiary companies, producing acreage, developed properties formerly non-producing, extended trans-

erating in Mexico, during 1935, had a daily average net production of approximately 5,400 barrels of crude oil. This crude was produced in part from owned oil and gas leases on approximately 495 acres, and in part from contractual interests in production from properties of others. Said subsidiaries also owned, at the year-end, undeveloped oil and gas leases on approximately 280,000 acres.

Penn Mex Fuel Co., 87.8% of whose capital stock is owned by Consolidated, produced approximately 2,000 barrels of crude oil net daily during 1935. This company, at the year-end, held oil and gas leases on approximately 49,000 acres located in Mexico, and undeveloped oil and gas leases on approximately 23,000 acres, on some of which drilling operations now are being conducted.

of a wholly-owned subsidiary at Parco, Wyo. Another small pipe line system owned by a wholly-owned subsidiary gathers Pennsylvania grade crude oil in Allegany and Steuben counties, N. Y. and transports it to refinery of such subsidiary at Wellsville, N. Y. Total crude oil pipe line mileage of wholly-owned subsidiaries in the United States at end of 1935 approximated 7,000 miles of trunk lines (a large proportion of which were parallel lines) and 7,000 miles of gathering lines.

Other oil transportation facilities of company include Sinclair Navigation Co., which, at December 31, last, owned 10 ocean-going tank ships for the transportation of crude oil and petroleum products, having a total deadweight tonnage of approximately 101,000 tons, and a total capacity of approximately 700,000 barrels.

Motorists ride 13 BILLION miles a year on SINCLAIR HC GASOLINE DOUBLE RANGE Anti-Knock

1/4 of all the oil used by AIR LINES in the U.S. is SINCLAIR Motor Oil

five far-sighted programs prepare companies for war

Far-sighted planning enhanced the ability of Sinclair companies to continue their growth through World War II. Almost as though the management possessed a crystal ball, it set in motion five programs in anticipation of the conflict which, by the system's twenty-fifth birthday year in 1941, had proven eminently correct. The sequence began with Hitler's rise to power in Germany.

First well in Venezuela 1941; find eased war shortages of crude oil

what Sinclair did:

● Sold its European marketing subsidiaries for cash and barter goods at a profit of about $1 million. So Sinclair lost nothing to Hitler during World War II.

● Anticipated the need for 100-octane gasoline by experiments with alkylation and polymerization processes beginning in 1937. When war came, Sinclair was able to expand quickly its production of aviation gasoline, the critically-needed polymers, and codimer.

● From 1937 stepped up oil exploration in Venezuela, with the result that the Santa Barbara field was discovered before U.S. entry into the war. By 1945 this new crude oil source contributed 27,000 barrels daily to U.S. operations, helping to offset acute shortages at home.

● Augmented its obsolete tankers with ten fast new vessels which were delivered in 1941 and 1942. Of these, 143,000 tons survived the war, giving Sinclair economical ocean transport during the post-war readjustment.

● Built a new products pipe line linking the eastern seaboard with the Ohio River serving the huge industrial cities of the Allegheny region and Washington, D.C. This line served Sinclair marketing when other transport was preempted for military uses.

Anticipating war, Sinclair sold all European outlets for $1,000,000 profit; unable to export money from Hitler Germany, company took iron pipe instead

Foresighted building of modern tanker fleet gave Sinclair ten efficient 15-knot vessels as World War II began; two were sunk on war duty

Combination crude and cracking unit at East Chicago substantially decreased fuel requirements for processing; efficiently produced gasolines for the home front

Expecting transport shortage, Sinclair built products pipe line in 1941 from Marcus Hook to Ohio River with spurs to Baltimore, Washington, D.C.

Arthur Godfrey, Sinclair announcer, opens terminal in nation's capital

Sinclair aids war industry in delivery of lubricants, aviation gasoline capacity

Sinclair's most conspicuous contribution to the war effort was the delivery of 100-octane fuel for airplanes. The entire industry's pre-war national output of this critical combat necessity was only 25,000 barrels a day. Sinclair alone constructed an identical volume during the first two war years. This record made Sinclair one of the largest producers of 100-octane gasoline.

The refineries also were important makers of military oils and greases, supplying 42 million gallons in 1944. Under the lash of war, many new demands were met by Sinclair to answer the needs of arctic and desert performance, six-mile high altitudes, and frictions never before encountered in jeeps, tanks and submarines.

A butadiene plant was built and operated for the U.S. Government to provide the raw materials for synthetic rubber. This achievement together with the know-how obtained in the production of polymers, codimer, isobutane, toluene, aviation alkylate, and exotic rearrangements of the versatile hydrocarbon molecule, gave Sinclair its start in the rich postwar field of petrochemicals.

An unsensational but equally vital contribution was the supply of 348 million gallons of navy fuel in 1944, and delivery of 450 million gallons of regular grade gasolines for military and government use.

This Houdry unit at Houston fed 2,000 bombing airplanes a day

Wellsville developed war lubricants for rugged sub-zero temperature use

Sinclair was a large war supplier of military lubricants; this Houston unit made special-purpose aviation oils for high altitude, long-range bombers

Sinclair built and operated butadiene plant for U.S. near Houston, exceeded 50,000 ton capacity by 30 percent

Fractionating unit, Marcus Hook, made enough toluene for 3,800 bombs daily

This polymerization plant at Marcus Hook produced components of high-octane gasoline also valuable in the big post-war automobile market

war-time marketing upsets services along home front as retail outlets shrink

The impressive war effort of the Sinclair operating companies was only 24 percent of their total business. The other 76 percent was service to the home front. Every normal marketing activity was deranged. War shortages caused oil to be delivered in glass containers and greases in cardboard. Hundreds of women were trained as "service aides" in retail stations. Rationing disrupted normal customer relations in gasoline and TBA sales.

Unprofitable outlets succumbed rapidly. By mid-1943 the total of company-owned and leased service stations had shrunk from 10,000 to 6,500, and independent franchises proportionately. But government regulation ended price wars and stabilized costs, while promotional expenses were negligible. As a result, net earnings averaged $21 million during the war years, a record at that time.

Fighting ship loads drummed Sinclair aviation gasoline in New York harbor

Six 17,000-ton tankers could travel unescorted, logged 330,000 war miles, delivered safely 147 million gallons of products

Eastern products pipe line linked to inland waterway at Steubenville, Ohio

Company's 6,000 tank cars, the industry's largest fleet, tracked 875 million miles during war with oil products for war plants, workers, farmers

unique terminal in Washington

The new products pipe line spurred retail growth throughout the middle Atlantic states, the Pennsylvania steel towns, and the nation's capital. Ability to deliver fuel oil to "keep the home fires burning," developed a major business of permanent importance. By Act of Congress, Sinclair thrust a products pipe line terminal into the District of Columbia.

The pipe line's Ohio River terminal permitted the line to be reversed, carrying mid-continent refined products, barged up the Mississippi, to the eastern industrial cities and to Sinclair's big pre-war marketing area. Thus in the stress of war, Sinclair was able to build for the return of peace.

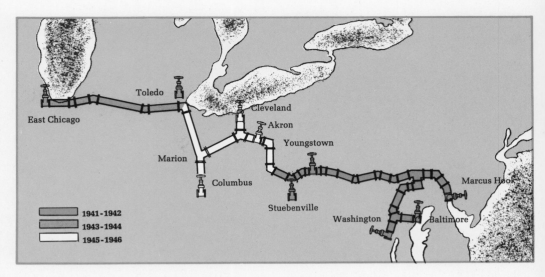

Products pipe line proved strategic, served home front over wide area

Home fuel business increased in war

Ability to deliver helped Sinclair service regular customers during war

$90,000,000 conversion makes fast transition to peace requirements

The war's sudden end exploded a hectic scramble to adjust to the oil products needs of a changed world. Two weeks after V-J Day, Sinclair's military deliveries were cut 75,000 barrels a day—about one-fifth of capacity. By the end of 1945, only six percent of Sinclair business was in war contracts.

Fortunately, the slack was absorbed by civilian demand. By 1947, the use of oil burners had vaulted 41 percent, natural gas 28 percent, space heaters 112 percent, compared to pre-war figures. Airplanes would soon begin to convert to jet propulsion and railroads to diesel engines. All this made prime commodities of such former Sinclair marginal products as diesel fuels, kerosene, natural gas and liquid petroleum gases. Millions of families moved to the suburbs. Farm mechanization swelled tractor energy by 59 percent. Motor boat service became a major industry. Sinclair had to adjust its refinery runs and its sales areas to the needs of a new age.

A further complication was the change in the refined products themselves. Due to war-developed capacity to make 100-octane fuels, aromatics and alkylates, aviation gasoline components lifted the octane numbers of automobile gasolines to a new high. Military-required research had created such novelties as all-weather lubricants, climate-tailored gasolines, long-lasting oils. These developments were harbingers of the petrochemical industry. At the same time, Sinclair's old pre-war friends had to be re-won, and an entire new generation wooed to the virtues of 1,200 products which now ranged from rocket lubricant to micro-crystalline wax.

Sinclair's management reacted quickly to the crisis. Five months after the war's end, a $90 million renovation was budgeted to adjust to the new conditions. Of this, $40 million was allocated to give the refineries greater flexibility, improved yields, and the quality needed to meet competition. Another $40 million was set aside for new service stations and terminals in the new suburbias. Extension of products pipe lines to the areas of rapid population growth was estimated to cost $10 million.

In the Thirtieth Anniversary year—1946— all this revitalization was under way. The company's name also was back on stream. During the war, the modern appellation for the holding company had emerged as Sinclair Oil Corporation.

Peace brought era of fierce readjustment to recapture and expand markets; (above) Detroit station before and after face-lift to attract new customers

Post-war costs trebled. Station at Anderson, South Carolina (upper) was built in 1929 for $9,824; in 1949 at Lakeland, Florida (lower) for $30,000

market area curtailed

In 1935, Sinclair marketed in most states, but much of this territory was unprofitable. The war-time abandonment of marginal facilities inspired a huge geographical retrenchment. By 1949, five southern states had been abandoned, and deep cuts had been made in sparsely settled areas. More than 900 service stations and 230 bulk plants were sacrificed, at a loss of 168 million gallons of annual sales. This shrinkage was overcome by the erection of 600 new stations a year in the mushrooming suburbias and on strategic highways, serviced by 35 economical terminals along products pipe lines. Farm business—slightly more profitable and less prone to price wars—was cultivated by elaborate promotional movies shown at rural fairs and gatherings.

The headlong reconversion to peace was given no breather by the national economy. Civilian demand actually jumped 20 percent over wartime volume. But the postwar inflation caught Sinclair's expansion program. From pre-war prices, pipe line construction was up $6,000 a mile. A refinery unit built for $5 million in 1940 now required an $8.5 million outlay. Deep well drilling costs doubled. Consequently, the capital expenditures for the five-year period 1946-1950 actually totalled $421,342,-000. In addition, employees received an 18 percent pay raise and many benefits. But the average retail gasoline price of 25.88 cents a gallon—up six cents from 1941 at the service station—left less profit than before. During this period, increased profits were chiefly the result of soaring sales volume.

National increase of 112 percent in home gas heating expanded Sinclair LPG production 183 percent in eight years; above, LPG storage in Seminole field

Costly television advertising pushed Sinclair products for mass audiences

Films and promotional programs aimed at farmers drew big-profit response

Struggle to regain markets stressed greater power and personal services

with profits at record, founder relaxes control after 33-year management

After 33 years of virtual one-man rule, the founder of the Sinclair enterprises relaxed his grip at the close of 1948. Record net earnings of $81 million climaxed Harry F. Sinclair's achievement. His was the most extensive petroleum complex to bear its founder's name. The post-war transition was complete. Refinery throughput averaged 258,500 barrels daily, crude oil production was nearly 40 million barrels a year at home and abroad. The pipe lines, one of America's largest systems, carried ten million barrels volume per month. The domestic market area contained 85 percent of the U.S. population. Oil production in Venezuela, sales in the Americas and Europe, attested to expanding international operations of an integrated structure. All this caused gross income in 1948 to cross half billion dollars a year for the first time at $636 million, or an average $2 million for each working day. On this peak Mr. Sinclair retired to California.

No one quite knew how the corporation had survived its first score of years, except on Mr. Sinclair's audacity. The financing, never adequate, during early 1920 had become precarious. A $50 million borrowing carried a 7½ percent interest rate. In addition, the proceeds were discounted by the bankers at 93½ percent, a shrinkage of $3.25 million. Yet the entire issue was redeemed within two years. Conversions to preferred stock at 104 retired about $20 million. The remainder was liquidated from proceeds of a new $50 million issue which bore a 7 percent coupon and a fifteen-year maturity. During the 1930-1935 depression, when many competitors succumbed, Sinclair doubled in size, and squeezed $143 million from its capitalization. But the country boy financing of the first two decades left management a debt burden which was onerous for another quarter century.

Mr. Sinclair's vision became reality at the most unlikely moment—the nadir of the depression in 1932. From then on, at least, the roof was on the house. After 1933, earnings and dividends were maintained. Never for a moment during his professional life had Mr. Sinclair surrendered his independence or that of his companies. The legacy he left was $700 million of assets for 99,500 stockholders, an employee staff of 21,000: an enormous enterprise. But more than that, he bequeathed the tradition of fierce independence upon which his successors would rely, and from which they, too, would draw their corporate strength.

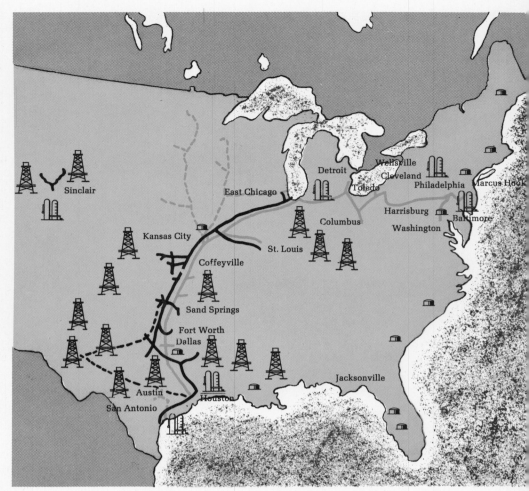

Founder Sinclair created America's largest, most economical pipe line system

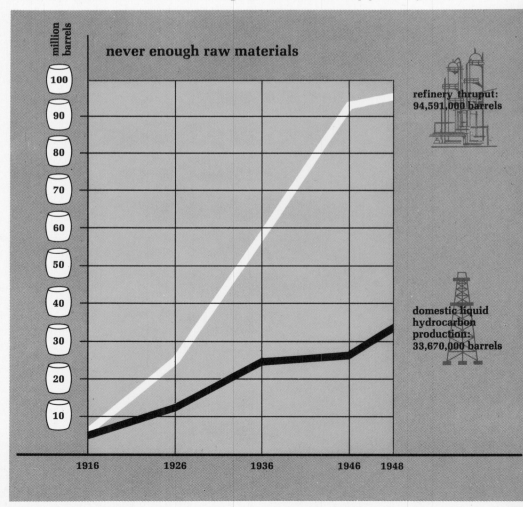

never enough raw materials

million barrels

refinery thruput: 94,591,000 barrels

domestic liquid hydrocarbon production: 33,670,000 barrels

1916 1926 1936 1946 1948

Gap between oil production and refinery capacity was Sinclair's big weakness

---

company's biggest problem: how to match oil supplies to appetite of refineries

" It takes all the running you can do," observed the Red Queen to Alice, "to keep in the same place. If you want to get somewhere else, you must run at least twice as fast as that."

Those responsible for providing Sinclair's crude oil requirements often felt like Alice in Wonderland: no matter how rapidly they brought in new oil field production, refinery throughput increased at a faster rate, so that proportionately crude oil supplies were out of balance. From 1920 to 1932, for example, crude oil production tripled, but sales quadrupled. Mr. Sinclair needed all available funds, and all he could borrow, to build refineries and to build or acquire pipe lines and marketing facilities. These items alone cost $300 million in cash and corporate stock between 1916 and 1933. The company's oil procurement policy was to buy—often as low as ten cents a barrel—in glutted new fields, then draw from storage when supplies were dear. An example: in 1924 Sinclair owned four million barrels of stored crude oil which had cost an average $1.53 a barrel. In addition, Sinclair Crude Oil Purchasing Company (50 percent owned by Sinclair) had 42 million barrels in storage. In 1926, when the price of mid-continent crude oil was $2.29, eight million barrels of the hoard were drawn off.

Another device was to race to the discoveries of others, buy proven leases from speculators, and develop them rapidly. Some of Sinclair's best properties were acquired in this way. In 1926 every available landman was rushed to Seminole on news of a successful wildcat, and in the next year the company produced seven million barrels of oil there. Similarly, Sinclair brought the second flowing well to the Oklahoma City field in 1929. Four months after the location by others of East Texas oil in 1930, Sinclair was in production, and in 1931 took 4.5 million barrels of crude oil from the new field. Aggressive buying

without costly wildcatting recovered all his purchase money in any field in two years, Mr. Sinclair told his bankers; after that, "everything is gravy."

This hand-to-mouth expediency was highly profitable when huge new flows inundated the midcontinent every few years, causing price upheavals from month to month and from field to field. But once the great finds had all been made, the older fields were stabilized, often under rigid withdrawal regulations. Additional production required enormous exploratory and development investment. Sinclair now was in trouble. During the decade 1935 to 1944, when all other major oil companies doubled their oil reserves, Sinclair's totals stood still, despite large increases in New Mexico and Wyoming. The average domestic yield of 26 million barrels yearly was about one-third of refinery throughput. Fortunately, 10 million barrels a year of imports from the Venezuela properties obscured the crisis during World War II. Wartime price-fixing also permitted the purchase of 38-gravity mid-continent crude for $1.17 a barrel, which was cheaper than exploration and development.

In 1949, with Mr. Sinclair retired as president, the crude oil shortage was acute. Sharp cutbacks in allowables under pro-

ration were effective in Texas and Oklahoma, where Sinclair produced 60 percent of its domestic supplies. These regulatory actions so curtailed productivity that Sinclair was able to produce only one barrel of oil for every three barrels of refinery throughput. The post-war open market price of crude oil shot to $1.62 a barrel in 1946 and $2.57 by the end of 1948. So Sinclair was paying an average $380,000 a day for 148,000 barrels of oil, on which the producer rather than Sinclair earned the profit.

As a partial offset to the crude oil squeeze, production of natural gasoline was pushed energetically, for blending with pipe line runs. The product was not subject to proration since it came from the wells with natural gas. Unfortunately, this supply also shriveled, from 109 million gallons in 1928 to 91 million in 1949. Sinclair also concentrated its exploration in Wyoming, Montana and Colorado which did not prorate production.

Only a genius for tight operation kept Sinclair competitive. To survive, Sinclair was required to refine, transport and market with the utmost efficiency, since its raw material costs were comparatively higher. This was the biggest problem Mr. Sinclair passed to his management heirs.

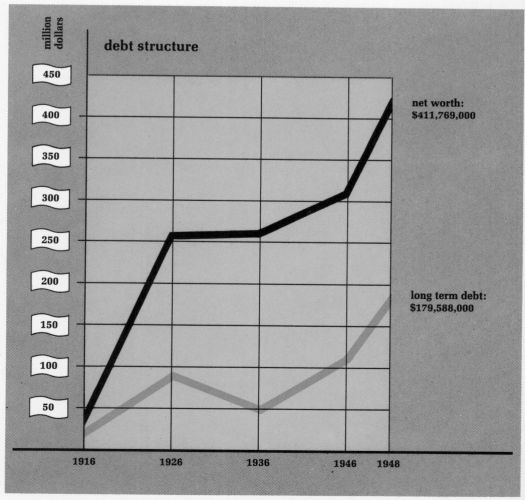

Early expansion amassed substantial debt, but net assets were impressive

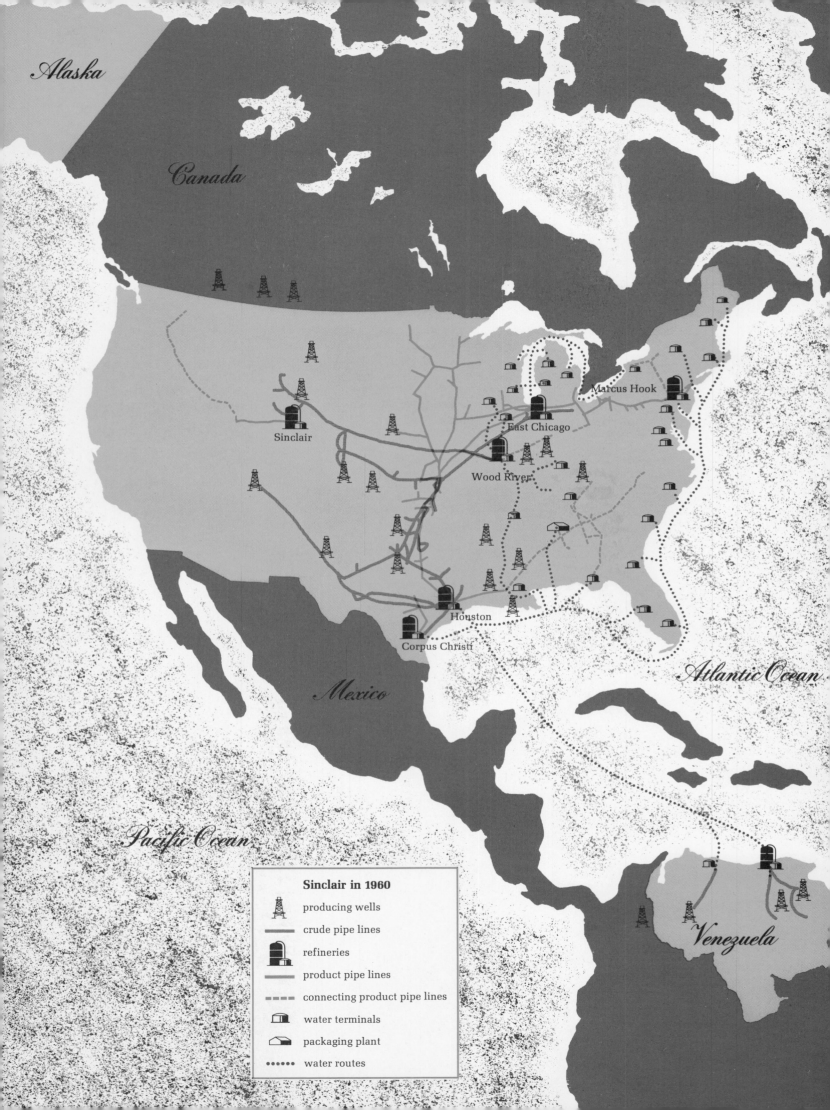

Alaska

Canada

Marcus Hook

Sinclair

East Chicago

Wood River

Houston

Corpus Christi

Mexico

Atlantic Ocean

Pacific Ocean

Venezuela

Sinclair in 1960

producing wells

crude pipe lines

refineries

product pipe lines

connecting product pipe lines

water terminals

packaging plant

water routes

twelve years of explosive growth

1949	1960
total assets	
$724,047,000	$1,486,567,000
sales and operating revenues	
$584,460,000	$1,222,383,000
sales of petroleum products (barrels)	
99,750,000	169,045,000
liquid hydrocarbons produced (barrels)	
39,127,000	66,899,000
natural gas produced (cubic feet)	
negligible	157,606,274,000
crude runs to refineries (barrels)	
95,109,000	159,569,000
petrochemical sales	
negligible	$26,700,000
pipe line deliveries, crude oil (barrels)	
92,027,000	162,800,000
pipe line deliveries, products (barrels)	
26,261,000	68,879,000
tanker and barge deliveries (barrels)	
54,350,000	91,500,000
research budget	
$3,722,000	$9,474,000

chapter 3:

the Spencer era: a time of change

Harry F. Sinclair passed management responsibility to the new generation in January 1949. His forceful, thirty-three-year leadership had not produced a management team. But in his fashion he had trained an heir. He had pushed Percy Craig Spencer along from legal counsel to corporate general counsel by 1946, to refining president in 1947, to corporate executive vice president in 1948, then to president and chief executive officer in 1949. Thus when Mr. Sinclair receded to the perimeter as chairman of the board, Mr. Spencer knew what he had to do.

"In a decade, he changed the character of the company."

decentralized management doubles sales and assets

Mr. Spencer's first necessity was to create a diversified management. He broke major operations into separate companies, decentralizing initiative and vesting operating authority in each subsidiary. Inspired by their independence, his colleagues bloomed creatively.

Another urgency was the need to secure Sinclair's share of the huge consumer buying which followed World War II. Annual national gasoline production jumped 77.1 percent, and household fuel use 109.3 percent in a decade. Merely to hold its prewar percentage of the petroleum products market, Sinclair was forced to expand its refining capacity.

A crash program increased refinery throughput 60 percent. This in turn motivated equivalent jumps in pipe line, storage and tanker capacities, plus hundreds of new marketing locations.

The expansion caused both gross sales and gross assets to double. But the old weakness—not enough crude oil—was not alleviated. At the end of 1956 Sinclair still bought, in an inflationary market, six of every ten barrels of crude oil it used. The competitive disadvantage was offset somewhat by the high sales volume, and by efficiency. The reorganized pipe line system had the industry's lowest ratio of expense to revenue; the waterborne fleet was as economical as any. The refineries achieved a utilization of 95 percent of capacity.

The capital expansion of Mr. Spencer's management cost $1,607,000,000 in twelve years. Of this, 88.5 percent was financed from cash income (net earnings, depreciation, depletion, etc). Thus the debt structure, though formidable, was placed on a firmer base than ever before.

1951: *move to new headquarters in New York symbolized changing times*

1949: *Harry F. Sinclair passed the command to P. C. Spencer after building in thirty-three years one of the nation's great industrial corporations*

1950-1951: *rapid modernization of purchased refinery at Wood River, Illinois, opened new mid-continent retail markets supplied by inland waterways*

1951: *tanker terminal, Jacksonville, Florida, rebuilt for efficiency and economy, was served by 13-knot tankers such as the 90,000-barrel capacity Sinclair Superflame*

1951: *first barge tow inaugurated economical transport on Mississippi, Ohio, Cumberland and Illinois rivers; by 1956 company operated four river tows plus two others on the Great Lakes*

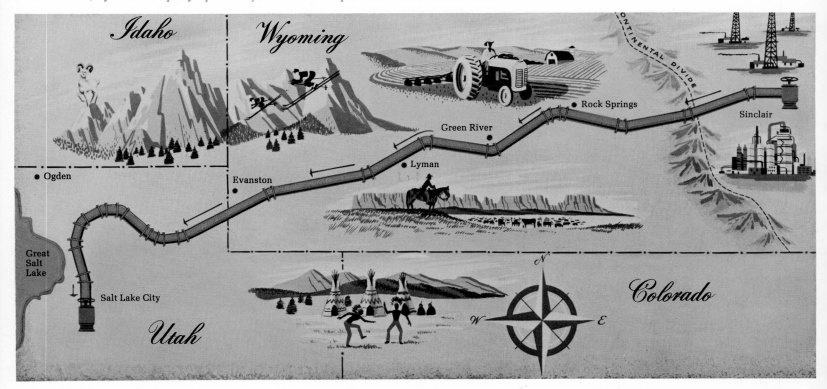

1953: *historic moment: Sinclair completed the first products pipeline to span the continental divide, linking Sinclair, Wyoming, refinery with Salt Lake City*

new coordination emerges

Mr. Sinclair had carried the company's future in his head: its plans were his dreams, its progress was his vision translated into action. Suddenly, as the master hand relaxed, the operating companies became a hatch of fledglings, each with its mouth wide open for more than its share of the budgetary diet. Mr. Spencer molded the various managements into teams independent in character yet coordinated for economy and corporate growth. Products research received greater emphasis with establishment of new laboratories at Harvey, Illinois. And Sinclair jumped ahead of many of its competitors in the development of a significant petrochemicals division.

1953: *advertising by billboards and newspapers was bolder, self-confident*

1949-1956: *clean-cut, strategically located stations expanded by 900 a year*

1958: *dealer meetings were bigger*

1960: *Sinclair's modern face in the marketplace presaged another change of command; the new designs were work of E. L. Steiniger, then President*

1959-1960: *28,000 outlets unveiled streamlined new marketing symbols*

conditions change again

In 1958 the post-war sellers' market waned. Fierce competition returned to the petroleum industry. Products prices deteriorated, harbinger of a long decline. Simultaneously, cuts in state crude oil lifting allowables forced Sinclair to spend $5,000,000 more for purchased crude oil between June and October. Mr. Spencer, his physical reorganization of the system completed, called now for a revaluation of Sinclair's future. This project was led by the parent company's new president, E. L. Steiniger. The era of expansion for bigness had ended.

An era of growth for profit, under Mr. Steiniger's direction, soon would emerge.

1955: $185,000 printing bill involved in American Republics Corp. purchase

Far-sighted thrust in petrochemicals increased total sales and profits

Huge costs of automated units encouraged group ventures for manufacturing or oil exploration; above, panel at Sinclair-Koppers styrene monomer plant

three critical areas of Spencer management

production

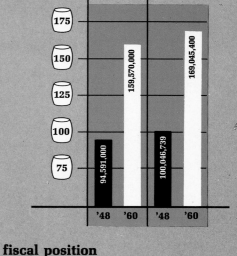

liquid hydrocarbons — '48: 45,041,000 / '60: 66,899,000 (million barrels)
natural gas — '48: 134,489,000 / '60: 157,606,000 (thousand cubic feet)

manufacture and sales

refinery thruput — '48: 94,591,000 / '60: 159,570,000 (million barrels)
net sales (all products) — '48: 100,046,739 / '60: 169,045,400

fiscal position

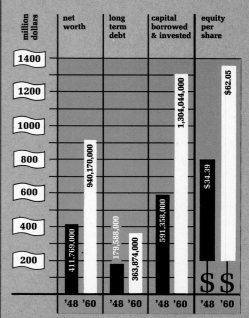

net worth — '48: 411,769,000 / '60: 940,170,000 (million dollars)
long term debt — '48: 179,588,000 / '60: 363,874,000
capital borrowed & invested — '48: 591,358,000 / '60: 1,304,044,000
equity per share — '48: $34.39 / '60: $62.05

By June 1961, when Mr. Steiniger became Chief Executive Officer, most of Mr. Sinclair's managers had retired. For the first time, Sinclair's highest echelon was largely composed of professionally educated executives: young veterans skilled in the new electronic and technological aids, the modern techniques and systems. With them, Mr. Steiniger led Sinclair into the third phase of its history: growth for profit

chapter 4:

Steiniger builds for greater profit

By 1958 the world-wide post-war sellers' market had abated. During these easy, prosperous years, Sinclair profits had reached a record $90.4 million in 1956. But motor gasoline prices then began a long decline (see chart below). The lower prices caught Sinclair in a bind, cutting sales income by $45 million in 1958. Increased costs in every department were aggravated by additional cash outlays for raw materials. Its historic low ratio of raw material production to refinery needs made Sinclair acutely sensitive to lower production allowables, to import restrictions on crude oil, and to price erosions. Sinclair moved promptly to offset the potential crisis. Early in 1957 E. L. Steiniger, a 32-year veteran, then chief of foreign operations, was elevated to a newly-created post of Executive Vice President, and charged with the responsibility of solving the burgeoning problems. Thus began a new emphasis which reached full tempo with Mr. Steiniger's elevation to the post of Chief Executive Officer in June 1961; he had been President since March 1958, a title he exchanged for that of Chairman of the Board in 1964, upon the naming of Executive Vice President Administration, O. P. Thomas, to the Presidency. The accent was no longer on physical growth, which had been achieved. Mr. Steiniger's goal was effective integration of the billion dollar family of companies to eliminate permanently the vexing imbalances which had plagued Sinclair's past, in an attempt to stabilize profit growth in the future. On September 30, 1957, Mr. Steiniger outlined his program to the principal executives. It was a 1-2-3 punch to knock out past problems and create a future champion. In essence, it was simple: **1) increase profit by reducing costs;**
2) realize greater profits from existing facilities;
3) create new sources of income.

3-point program offsets effect of low prices:

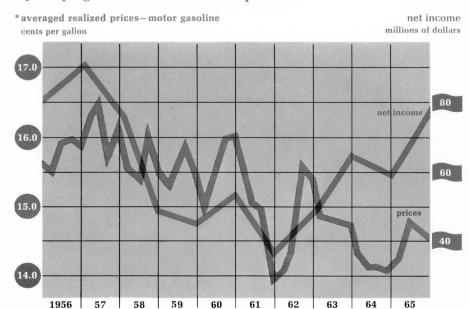

*averaged realized prices—motor gasoline
cents per gallon

net income
millions of dollars

*Average prices realized by Sinclair...last three months estimated

attacks on expenses generate economies of major significance

"Don't fight the uncontrollables such as weather, price wars and prorationing," Mr. Steiniger told his associates. "Let's counteract their effects with better performance." The first prong of his 1-2-3 attack was an "immediate and relentless" reduction in costs. By 1965 this belt-tightening had produced savings reckoned in the millions of dollars.

The achievement was aided greatly by Sinclair's first large-scale use of computers. Electronically-programmed studies refined the established general guide lines and indicators for successful retrenchments and economies. The computers became tools to speed management decisions by fast collection and analysis of complicated data. The Sinclair Optimization System (SINOPSYS) was developed to lower costs and to improve profit margins on refined products.

The next step in computer use was the development of automated equipment, and computerized systems and methods, which generated further measurable savings. Sinclair introduced the industry's first automated pipe line system in 1965, and made a start that year toward programmed control of refinery operations and some petrochemical processes. In crude oil production, nearly half of all raw material measuring units had been mechanized by 1965.

Crude oil purchase policies were changed. Refiners specified the types of raw materials which computer studies showed they needed for the most economical production of more profitable products. In manufacturing, electronic precision whittled the per barrel unit refining cost. Fuel and power bills were cut by the use of more efficient equipment and the selection of most economical fuels. Greater refining efficiency caused no loss in production when Sinclair disposed of its plants at Corpus Christi and Wellsville for a net operational saving of $1.5 million a year.

marketing costs reduced

Marketing costs were slimmed through economies projected by Mr. Steiniger's Planning Department. The emphasis here was on pinpoint profit realizations at the tank wagon level. Marketing economics studies pared 2,000 unprofitable service stations, and also resulted in bulk plant consolidations. Deliveries were rerouted to save freight. New stations and bulk plants were located for long term growth in highest sales concentration areas. Sinclair's huge transportation system was overhauled. Its railroad tank car fleet, the industry's largest, was sold. A new tanker design was pioneered, reducing normal operating costs. These improvements, with the pipe line modernizations, enabled Sinclair to move record volumes of raw materials and products at lower per mile costs. Also, pipe line bottlenecks were removed, to route various type crude oils to the refineries most efficiently equipped to use them. Even the research laboratories were asked to produce cash crops, and did so.

As a result of these economies—and more efficient use of manpower—Sinclair in 1964 handled 179 million barrels of sales with fewer employees than had been required in 1950 on a volume of 116 million barrels.

work programs expose hidden extravagances

By 1963 the obvious economies were in effect. Mr. Steiniger then challenged management to rout out the hidden or long-

Savings start with plans. Here President O. P. Thomas, who pioneered computerized work functions for Sinclair, presides at the decision to automate the processing of Sinclair's 1,500,000 credit card accounts. Such a change required intricate liaison between the functions of employee and community relations; finance; planning; the corporate secretary's office; the comptroller's department and chief administrative officer

entrenched extravagances. Tighter budgets inspired a search for even greater savings, and a larger return from every piece of equipment and every employee. A Profit Plan and Expense Budget scrutinized every detail of the business for profit improvement. Many accounting, purchasing and other administrative procedures duplicated among the subsidiaries were consolidated. Many field offices were combined. Computer centers mechanized hundreds of work functions, and processed data for fast answers to work-a-day inquiries. Clerical details were automated in payroll handling, raw materials purchases, credit card handling, the processing of dividend payments, and even the storage and plotting of geological data used in foreign and domestic oil field exploration. Computations too intricate for the more modest processing centers were synchronized with the big IBM 7044 in New York.

Each new step in the economy drive led, as expected, to the disclosure of hidden opportunities for savings, or suggested new sources of revenue. Altogether, the self-scrutiny and tightening of the entire enterprise contributed greatly to Sinclair's profit comeback. Earnings bulged 32 percent in 1962, and again by an identical percentage in 1963, despite the problem of declining products prices.

Industry's first automatic loading devices for LP-Gas transfer gave Sinclair dealers 24-hour unattended service, also cut Sinclair's costs

Reason for the change. Credit card processing extended the usefulness of Sinclair's new Computer Center (above) in Chicago. This new data processing unit also services marketing accounting operations for the western region

The final step. Personnel are trained in highly skilled procedures for accurate transfer of individual credit card records to data processing units

greater creative uses of existing resources extend profit margins

The second cutting edge of Mr. Steiniger's profit-building program fashioned more creative uses from Sinclair's resources. The objective was greater dollar return on the existing $1.5 billion of assets. An outstanding success of this drive was the development of $61.5 million in new sales revenue from petrochemicals by 1964—a figure later exceeded in a program involving highly imaginative low-risk expansion (see chapter 5).

Equally ingenious if less sensational was a new philosophy of manufacturing. Sinclair broke away from the traditional adjustment of refinery product mix to sales and seasonal demands for such items as heating fuels. Instead, runs were geared the year around to optimal gasoline output,

emphasizing greatest potential profit. Such a policy enabled Sinclair's engineers to increase the percentage of light oil products derived from a barrel of crude oil. This meant an additional 294 million gallons yearly of products sold as higher-valued gasolines and jet fuels.

Another outstanding operation increased by 83.5 percent between 1959 and 1964 the revenues received from the sale of natural gas and LPGs (so-called bottled gases). Mr. Steiniger personally spurred gas sales, dubbing them "Sinclair's very important cash crop." Natural gas production nearly doubled, from 396 million cubic feet a day in 1959 to 709 million in 1964. Sinclair's marketing of LP-Gas was extended to many states. Greater emphasis was placed on the extraction of liquid hydrocarbons in the field for profitable blending with refinery stocks, and further upgrading into petrochemicals at Lyondell. Such production reached a record 23,866 net barrels daily in 1964. The natural gasoline production, plus refining economies, reduced significantly the raw

materials Sinclair needed to buy, for another saving.

The recovery of more crude oil from older fields, with sizable increases in reserves—much cheaper than finding new oil fields—was pushed through better secondary recovery methods researched in Sinclair's laboratories. Also, participation in 87 new field unitization programs from 1962 to 1964 added an estimated 95 million barrels of recoverable crude oil to reserves. At the same time, acreage was pruned substantially. Many costly unproductive leases were eliminated. Large reservoirs of previously shut in and therefore unproductive gas resources in Oklahoma and Canada were sent to market in 1963 and 1964. In addition, pipe line connections to the rapidly-expanding market areas around Denver gave new sales outlets for refined products from the Sinclair, Wyoming, refinery.

Greater attention also was given to a larger return from brainpower. In 1962 a Management Development Center was opened.

Petrochemical expansion generates new business and responsibilities for many operations. Involved are the production and purchase of various types of crude oil and gases and their delivery by pipe lines to manufacturing units; the refining of specified by-products at various refineries; capital costs; sales to foreign customers. Here the logistics of greater profits from butadiene manufacture are charted by officers representing the parent company, refining, crude oil production, petrochemicals, pipe lines, and economic evaluation. All individual operations must be coordinated to bring about the desired result: greater profits from existing resources

It encouraged employees to develop their intellectual resources for greater self-satisfaction and for larger contributions to Sinclair.

new marketing ideas
widen sales outlets

An upheaval in marketing techniques accompanied the drive for greater profits. Sinclair's public image—its signs, symbols and service outlets—was redesigned to improve prestige. Several smaller marketing subsidiaries were merged into Sinclair Refining Company, the principal marketing subsidiary. Researchers gave the marketers a better product in nickel-additive fuels, thus attracting new customers. Big sales volume truck-stop and traveler one-stop roadside complexes replaced some retail outlets. A significant increase in revenues is being achieved by direct retailing of fertilizers to farmers from Sinclair's share of the Calumet Nitrogen Products Company plant, and by the formation in 1965 of a plastics partnership known as Sinclair-Koppers Company.

New petrochemical ventures and other profit-building programs must conform to the almost countless rules and regulations of Government bodies, foreign and domestic. Here, Chairman E. L. Steiniger and President O. P. Thomas confer with counsel on legal aspects of contemplated operations

Decision of the meeting (left) causes production modifications at Sinclair's impressive Lyondell, Texas, petrochemical complex, a few miles from the Houston refinery which supplies most of the basic feed stocks. Picture above shows the methyl-ethyl-ketone unit, new in 1964, which makes solvents for plastics

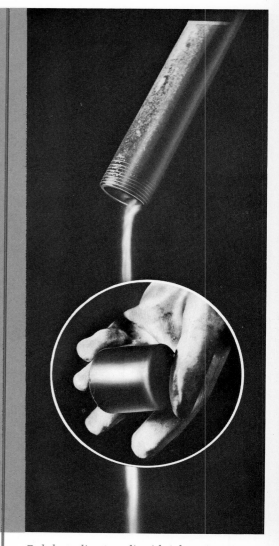

Polybutadiene, a liquid (above) hardens into urethane rubber (in glove), or is potentially useful in solid rocket fuels, foam rubber, adhesives, plastic novelties, etc.

for greater stability third phase attacks traditional weaknesses

The third phase of Mr. Steiniger's 1-2-3 profit program—to create lucrative *new* sources of income—entailed an important change in management philosophy. "Let's budget," the chief executive said, "on the basis of what we need the most, not on how much money we have to spend." This change forced planners to give priority in the expenditure of capital funds to the correction of Sinclair's major weaknesses —such as the low output of crude oil from its own wells. Management sought a truly balanced integration of operations to achieve permanent stability, and make Sinclair less sensitive to gasoline price fluctuations.

Closing the gap between raw materials production and refinery throughput received first priority. A current record high ratio of 53 percent was reached in January 1965. (See graph, chapter 10.) With new discoveries and increasing production in Canada, Colombia, and Algeria, acquisitions which added production from Peru and Libya, and increased domestic output, Sinclair's total net production of raw materials rose dramatically from an average of 204,000 barrels a day in 1963 to a rate of about 250,000 net barrels daily as 1965 came to a close. Also significant to Sinclair's future are certain producing properties acquired subject to reserved produc-

tion payments. The liquidation of certain of these production payments in 1965 should add an estimated 1,000 barrels daily of crude oil and 24 million cubic feet of gas daily to Sinclair's resources. By 1976, when all current production payments are expected to expire, an estimated daily 20,000 barrels of liquids and 212 million cubic feet of gas should be added to domestic output from these sources alone.

diversification policy defined

Sinclair's activities which produced chemicals for direct retail highest profit sales levelled attention on Mr. Steiniger's policy of diversification, first articulated formally in 1962. The development of farm markets for Sinclair-produced fertilizers, and the organization of a plastics venture, the Sinclair-Koppers Company, by 1965 had surged Sinclair's petrochemicals into a $100 million a year business. Sinclair was committed to wide diversification *within* petroleum-oriented fields, to broaden and stabilize the profit base; but expansion was not contemplated into industries unsuited to Sinclair's management experience and practical know-how. Thus diversification is within the industry, and not into outside unfamiliar enterprises. Stability of income was paramount in the huge petrochemical expansion (see chapter 5). Also, to increase petrochemical profitability, products were constantly upgraded, existing plants and equipment were utilized more efficiently and profitably, and new plants were added.

in summary

Progress of the three-pronged policy:

1961: the low point. Lowest prices and earnings in 15 years were accompanied by increases in raw materials and gas production, and a 15.8 percent rise in export sales.

1962: the road back. New record in refined products sales resulted from upgraded quality. Earnings increased $11.4 million despite a $12 million shrinkage in price realizations.

1963: further progress. Net profit rose 32 percent despite falling prices, all but $300,000 of the gain attributed to the 1-2-3 program.

1964: a pause to regroup. Prices at a ten-year low. But of $20.4 million withering of price realizations, all but $4 million were offset by the 1-2-3 results. Year 1964 marked a lull between the full impact of completed retrenchments, and the earnings leverage generated by new programs.

1965: the rising tide. Earnings begin sharp rise in response to management program, and higher goals are set for future.

Here, the manager of project development for Sinclair International, poses a problem in the delivery and marketing of substantially increased quantities of crude from Sinclair discoveries in Algeria and wells in Libya. Involved are foreign sales, international administration, transportation and supply, manufacturing, and marine transportation

Post-war American enthusiasm for yachting provides important new sources of revenue; above, Sinclair's exclusive marina at 1964-1965 N. Y. World's Fair

Nickel additive for gasolines contributed greater profits for 1964

Discovery in 1962 of Rhourde el Baguel opened a new continent to Sinclair. Here Board Chairman E. L. Steiniger (left) and F. A. Bush, Sinclair International Oil Company President, examine production manifold which collects crude oil from many wells into single flow line

Mr. Steiniger in Libya reads flow meter which measures daily production of crude oil in which Sinclair owns about a one-fourth interest

chapter 5:

research:
a practical affair

At Sinclair, scientific research is older than the parent corporation or any of its operating companies. This anomaly results from Harry F. Sinclair's acceptance of a research project in 1916 several months before the formal organization became effective. The urgency then was a refining process to distill more gasoline from crude oil.   Like the original program, which successfully created the Isom still and made Sinclair competitive with the industry's best, research has emphasized practical results: to earn money, to save money, to evolve original or improved commercially lucrative products and systems. From the laboratories have flowed hundreds of salable items, including important industry "firsts." The technological achievement has been equally significant. The scientists and engineers have produced complete refinery units, pipeline and marine transport advances and economies, automation systems, and new processes and equipment for wildcatting and the secondary recovery of crude oil. From research has come a giant scion of the corporation: a major venture in petrochemistry. In sum, for fifty years Sinclair research has been, and continues to be, a critical impetus to Sinclair's growth.

Nuclear radiation cave protects scientist testing radioactive substances, at Harvey, Illinois. Sinclair laboratories by 1965 occupied ten ultramodern buildings at Harvey and a large new laboratory at Tulsa. Compare with company's first research lab at right: East Chicago refinery, 1918.

"Bug Row" at Coffeyville becomes campus at Harvey

"Nobody makes better products from oil than does Sinclair," the company told its employees in 1919. The same boast might be trumpeted at the Fiftieth Anniversary, due to stellar research and—equally important—aggressive management exploitation of scientific results. Research has always been the tool of the salesmen, not an esoteric independent operation.

For the first 35 years, the refining company maintained the laboratories, although from 1921 onward problems were solved for the pipeliners, from 1926 for the marine department, and from 1932 for all subsidiary companies. But the mainstream of scientific endeavor concentrated for two decades on systems and processes to refine better gasolines and oils.

Research began at Coffeyville, Kansas. There the first Sinclair company absorbed a "bug row" at the Cudahy refinery. A two-man project by W. H. Isom and engineer John Bell was continued to find a new process for cracking the middle distillates of crude oil into larger volumes of gasoline. In 1917, "bug row" was transferred to the new refinery at East Chicago. It remained there until completion of the "campus environment" laboratories at Harvey, Illinois, in 1948. Three years later, the parent corporation reorganized research into a separate company. In 1952, Sinclair separated from Harvey the scientific study of crude oil exploration, the secondary recovery of oil from older wells, and the conservation of oil resources. This new arm of research was housed in temporary quarters at Tulsa until the dedication of the Tulsa Research Center in 1963.

Cable driller scorned science, knew from "feel" of cable what was underground

Earliest laboratory was isolated by fence in corner of East Chicago refinery

Isom's famous still. Left, first pilot plant; right, earliest full scale refinery unit, both at East Chicago

1938: machine to test effects of motor oils on engine bearings and piston rings
1954: apparatus to measure adsorption of gases by solids at Harvey, Illinois

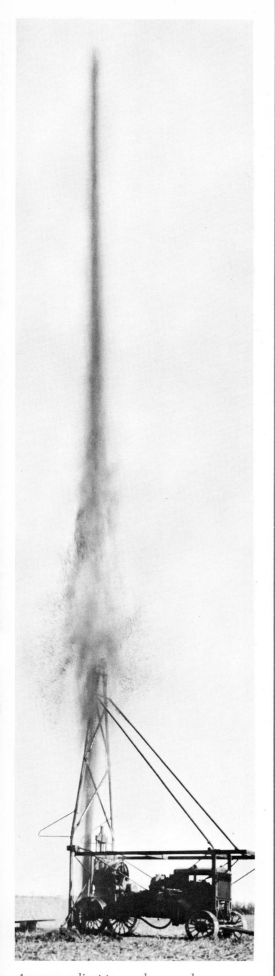

Among earliest to employ geophysics, a Sinclair test in Oklahoma in 1932 fired 1,786 reflection and 531 refraction shots from 110 locations

Research and Development Dept., East Chicago, 1932; and at Harvey, Illinois, 1948

versatile programs yield conspicuous achievements

Among the most conspicuous successes of Sinclair research are these:

1919: the Isom still doubled the amount of gasoline obtained from crude oil

1926: H-C was the industry's first premium grade high octane gasoline

1931: acid-treating gave Sinclair forefront position in aviation lubricants

1935: TENOL was the first successful additive diesel lubricating oil

1940-1944: war effort produced catalytic cracking units for aviation gasoline; also, the design and operation for U.S. government of a butadiene plant

1947: rust inhibitor RD-119 introduced in gasoline and heating oils heralded later additive trend in oil industry

1948: pioneer studies initiated to recover crude oil from depleted fields by underground combustion techniques

1953: first regenerative platinum reforming catalyst developed to manufacture high octane gasoline and petrochemicals

1954: oil from oil shale pioneered by underground combustion methods

1956: X-chemical added to Power-X gasoline, reduced preignition of engines

1963: DINOSEIS (see picture) announced; also, rocket engine lubricant for space vehicles

1964: pipe line company research perfected industry's first closed loop system for automatic computer control of entire pipe line from Cushing, Oklahoma, to East Chicago...new nickel compound developed and used in DINO and DINO SUPREME gasolines to reduce engine wear, carburetor icing, and preignition

1965: new DUOTREAT process created exclusive line of highly refined lubricants and special products

Between 1920 and 1925 Sinclair research cost two million dollars. By 1930 the tab was a million dollars a year; by 1965 it was 15 million dollars a year. The research staff which numbered two in 1916 spawned to 100 by 1928, 500 by 1948, 755 by 1965. U.S. patents in force: in 1919, one; in 1951, 360; in 1961, 573; in 1965, more than 700.

Ten buildings at Harvey permit 575 scientists to departmentalize their facilities with ideal space and equipment

Carburetor icing measured by this unit in nickel additive development

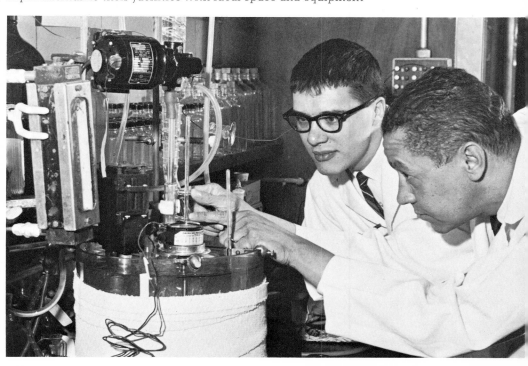

One of 46 Ph.D. scientists at Harvey checks experiment with young assistant

Developed by Tulsa, machine trademarked DINOSEIS generates seismic shock waves, records results for computer analysis, eliminates dynamite shootings

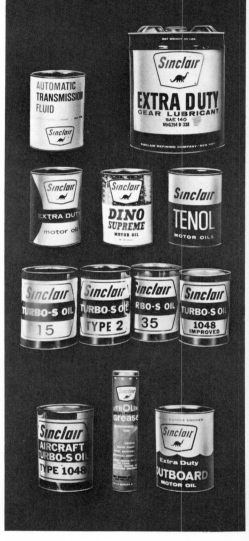

Roominess at Harvey allows indoor construction of big pilot plants and prototypes for refinery units; here, a fluid catalytic cracker built in 1951

Sinclair announces the most important gasoline improvement since World War II

Exclusive Nickel Compound 10 times more effective than other additives in combating harmful engine deposits!

petrochemicals contribute big growth, larger profit

At the Fiftieth Anniversary, petrochemicals accounted for almost 10 percent of Sinclair's gross income, and contributed significantly to profits. Sinclair Petrochemicals, Inc., organized in 1952, was the fastest growing member of the family, its expansion rate 15 to 20 percent a year. Revenue from petrochemicals was a response to management's emphasis on finding new profit sources in the versatile petroleum molecule, deriving more profit from each barrel of crude oil, and diversifying within the industry.

Sinclair's development into a leader in petrochemicals was not the result of shotgun hit or miss activity. It was a cautious progression from one carefully planned project to another. The trend is away from the simpler hydrocarbons—now in oversupply—to intermediate organic chemicals, plastics, balanced fertilizers, and other important chemical process-industry items.

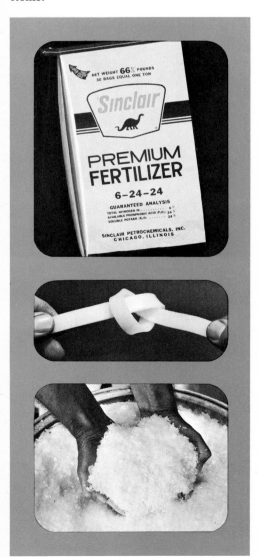

Three of the best: agricultural fertilizer, a new product; DINOFIN, a flexible wax polymer of great versatility; styrene maleic anhydride base stock

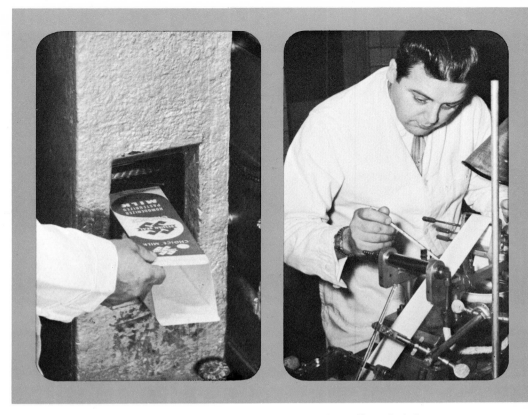

Tests using wax polymer to develop high gloss coated cardboard (left) paper (right) with wax on one side, polyethylene coating on reverse

Pipelines from underground storage of liquid petrochemicals in salt dome near Houston, Texas, lead to cylindrical and spherical tanks at Lyondell

Sinclair is a major manufacturer of paraxylene, a basic petrochemical

Tight automated control at Lyondell keeps costs down, contributes to company's profitability in petrochemical production and sale

Installation of catalytic reformers started the surge in petrochemicals

Automation (upper photo) controls (below) a methyl-ethyl-ketone unit which produces a solvent used in de-waxing lubricating oil stocks

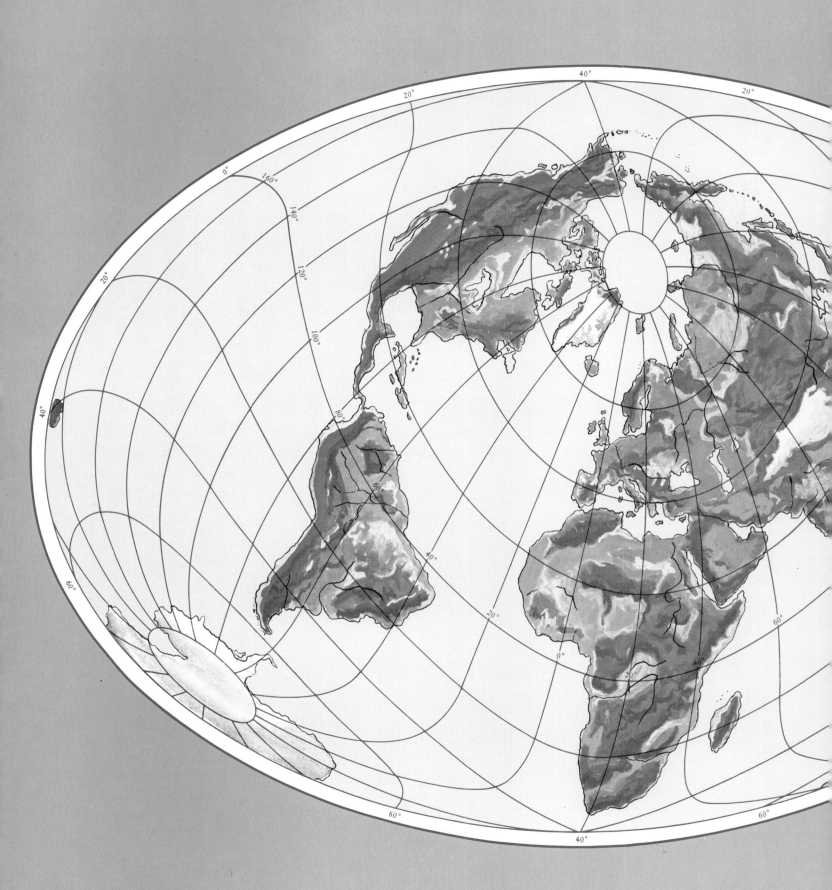

chapter 6:

foreign operations: global in trend

Aggressive gains in foreign crude oil production and markets have added a new dimension to Sinclair operations in recent years. To existing reservoirs in Venezuela and Canada have been added important crude oil discoveries in Colombia, Algeria and Nigeria, and an acquisition in Libya. At or near capacity operation of the Venezuelan refinery, chiefly for Latin American and European markets, plus vigorously promoted sales of petroleum, refined products and petrochemical stocks in Europe, have extended Sinclair's profit opportunities to four continents. The story in a capsule: 1961-1964: foreign crude oil production, including Canada, up 41 percent and natural gas up 200 percent; overseas sales up 100 percent.

As the search for oil expands to almost inaccessible jungles, deserts and arctic wastes, portable equipment suitable for airlift is mandatory. Here, lightweight seismographic shot hole drill in operation

failures in Baku and Iraq, success in South America

Sinclair's first foreign venture, in Mexico, had recovered only 75 percent of the $40 million investment before the expropriation of 1938. The remainder was recovered later in the form of crude oil by an agreement with the Mexican government. The 1920s also produced three romantic interludes exciting for what might have been. Mr. Sinclair negotiated an extensive concession in the rich Iraq middle east; the contract was not executed, however, when Mr. Sinclair's Mammoth Oil Company became involved in the Teapot Dome controversy. In 1923, Mr. Sinclair and retinue, on a $250,000 trip to Russia, obtained agreement with the Soviets to develop the fabulous Baku field in the Crimea; but the contract never was honored. In recompense, the Russians gave Sinclair a concession on Sakhalin Island, which had an estimated 3.36 billion barrels of oil; but in 1924 the Japanese, disputing Soviet sovereignty of the territory, jailed and then deported a Sinclair geology party, ending the adventure. Also in the 1920s, $4,000,000 was dropped in futile drillings in Angola, Portuguese West Africa.

More successful was an exploration of Venezuela, begun in 1926. By 1939 this had cost $7,300,000. More intensive effort then discovered the Santa Barbara field in 1941 which, by the Fiftieth Anniversary, had yielded 87 million barrels of oil. The nearby Guere field was found in 1950, and Barinas, far inland, in 1953. Venezuelan operations since 1960 have contributed liberally to annual net earnings. To the west, Sinclair in 1960 struck oil in Colombia which, by 1965, brought Sinclair 7,000 barrels of production daily.

Venezuelan refinery as it went on stream in 1950; with a 36,000-barrel daily throughput, it yields refined products for Latin America and Europe

Earliest foreign refinery; original Isom still was erected in Cuba, 1919

Historic moment: Sinclair's M. L. Gosney loads first crude delivered by new 211-mile pipe line from Barinas field to Venezuelan seaport, Nov. 22, 1957

1959: Sinclair geologist in Colombia

Discovery well in Provincia Field, Colombia, 1960, 25% Sinclair-owned, cost $1,000,000; this field yields company 7,000 barrels daily of crude oil

Flown-in bulldozer cuts jungle road

Every oil prospector has this photo

Automation overseas: automatic tank farm and pipe line installations cut production and maintenance costs in Provincia Field of Colombia's jungles

Sinclair is part of many communities

international subsidiary generates growth abroad

The ascent of E. L. Steiniger to the post of chief executive officer in 1961 quickened appreciably the tempo of foreign operations. Mr. Steiniger made the organization world-conscious for the first time, with the creation in 1961 of Sinclair International Oil Company. This subsidiary was charged to develop crude oil production and products sales outside the American continent. Sales, chiefly in Europe, vaulted 36.9 percent in 1963 and jumped 28 percent more in 1964, including export petrochemicals, the sales of which doubled in 1964.

Africa became an important producer of crude oil for Sinclair as the Fiftieth Anniversary neared. In Algeria, Sinclair as operator discovered in 1962 the Rhourde el Baguel field. In Nigeria, a wildcat struck oil in 1964. Exploration continued on a 38-million acre concession in Somalia. An acquisition gave Sinclair an important position in Libya, and a small marketing-producing position in Peru in December 1964. From all these sources, plus Venezuela and Colombia, Sinclair's foreign production (excluding Canada) leaped to 78,000 net barrels daily at the beginning of 1965, up 33.3 percent from the 1964 daily average.

Far-flung oil search rockets costs. Discovery well in Algerian desert, 1962, 28% Sinclair-owned, required air-conditioned camp for engineers, drillers

Rhourde el Baguel, Algeria. Water pond for drilling operation attracted camels from within a hundred miles; in the desert, water is shared by all

Somali longshoremen crew bosses pose on beach during lightering operation

Oil prospectors expect the expensively unusual; without harbors or roads, oil equipment and daily sustenance for crews exploring 38 million acre Somalia concession must be lightered to exposed beaches, airlifted inland

three Canadian provinces swell oil and gas yields

Sinclair followed the oil trail to Canada late in 1949 through a new subsidiary of the domestic producing company. Little more than geological survey was attempted until a wildcat was drilled in Alberta's Joarcam area in 1952. This success stimulated a wider play. By the end of 1954, three Alberta fields had become producers, and in 1955, with others, the Lator wildcat opened a new oil region.

The bleak northwest, matted with treacherous tundra in summer and frozen in winter, was penetrated in 1957. Large leases were secured in Saskatchewan and British Colombia. Here also exploration was pressed, and production obtained in the PeeJay and Boundary Lake oil fields and the Beg gas area.

By Sinclair's Fiftieth Anniversary, oil and natural gas wells were in production in the three westernmost Canadian provinces. The consistently swelling volume by 1965 totalled 12,000 barrels of oil daily and 15 million cubic feet of gas. These were substantial additions to western hemisphere operations, and opened new market outlets both in Canada and western United States.

Sinclair's discovery well in Canada, the Julius Olsen No. 1 near Edmonton, Alberta, 1952, still produces crude oil as part of unitized operation

Cricket pumps at ten degrees below zero in Swan Lake field, Edmonton, Alberta

Alaska highway milepost 128 locates Sinclair-operated natural gas field

This 1958 discovery and 22 other wells received pipe line connections in 1962

Drilling platform in Cook Inlet, Alaska; State looms large in Sinclair's future.

these early conditions are gone forever...

1917: DeQueen, Ark., ditching by hand

1916: how to light a nitro shot fuse

1918: firing a still with gasoline

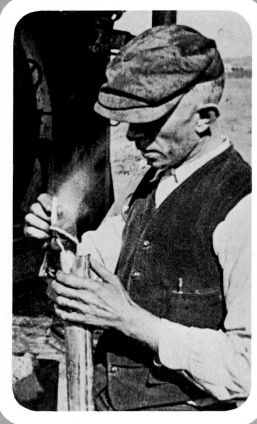

1919: employee lunch room, E. Chicago

1917: bunk house, Coal City, Illinois

1924: workers' change house, Wellsville

919: up-to-date forge, E. Chicago

919: family housing, Cushing field

chapter 7:

the employee story

When in 1929 Sinclair offered its employees a group insurance program, the plan was unusually enlightened for its time. It included monthly income for permanently disabled workers. Since then, Sinclair has maintained attractive pension and other welfare benefits. Since 1934, Sinclair has negotiated on a master agreement covering union employees in production, pipe line, refinery and certain research operations. More than 150 contracts involve other operations. 🦕 🦕 By the Fiftieth Anniversary, employee benefits embraced retirement annuities, extended medical, hospital and surgical services, generous wage continuance during illness, incentives to savings, liberal paid vacations, and tuition and other aids to education and self-improvement. Working conditions were among the best in the petroleum world, due to Sinclair's postwar modernization of every operating subsidiary. Through judicious management, Sinclair's total payroll in comparison with gross income was among the smallest of major American companies; but its per-employee return in wages and benefits was among the highest, well above the national averages.

**sales generated per employee
high in dollar volume**

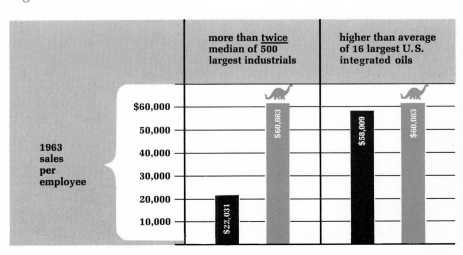

	more than <u>twice</u> median of 500 largest industrials	higher than average of 16 largest U.S. integrated oils

1963 sales per employee: $22,031 vs $60,083 | $58,009 vs $60,083

employee rewards up 400 percent in a single generation

"Our yardstick," Mr. Sinclair once told his stockholders, "is a fair day's pay for a fair day's work." But to him, this platitude meant that employee families enjoy wages that are among the highest paid by American industry. The evolving social concept of corporate concern for a balanced system of company social security has found Sinclair still "among the highest." Sinclair families in 1963 had a $260 a-month larger income and benefits return than the U.S. national annual average of $5,190. Sinclair's payrolls in the U.S. alone that year were $142 million. In addition, contributions to employee benefit programs totalled $18 million, or about $75 a month per worker.

Back in 1932, the year Sinclair emerged as a great industrial enterprise, the investment per employee was $18,000 in plant and equipment. Technological advances have caused a 20 percent■ drop in employee numbers from the all-time peak of 1957. But the new technology gives much better jobs to more skillful people. The investment per employee has jumped 396.5 percent■ since 1932, to $71,377 per employee■; in the same time the average economic reward has vaulted 400 percent■ from $1,665 yearly to $8,333■ in pay and benefits.

■as of December 31, 1963

Self-improvement program offers free foreign language instruction classes

Glaring lights, a high stooled bench, a metal cage (top) adorned Wellsville accounting·office in 1926; compare with today's bright quarters in New York

Truck, left, was deluxe equipment at Seminole natural gasoline plant in 1929; modern installations feature built-in instant control fire systems

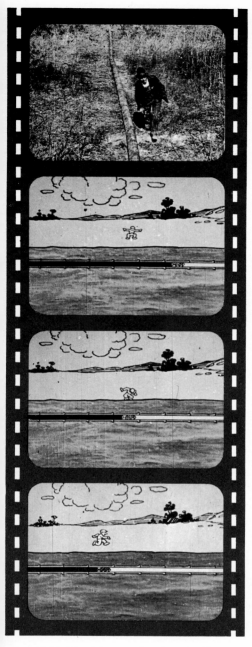

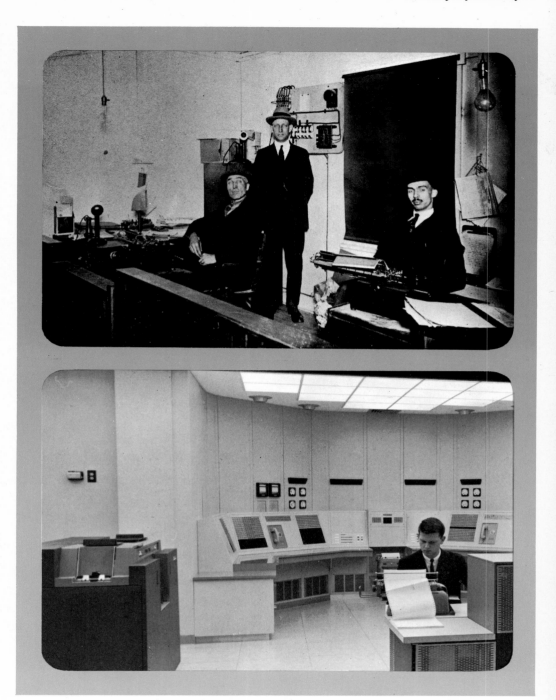

In a 1921 Sinclair movie, the pipeliner sprinted three miles an hour to track go-devil; with stamina he lasted nine miles; if pipe clogged, he opened it. Modern cleaners travel unaccompanied

From pipe line stations 40 miles apart telegraphers in 1916 controlled hand valve operations; modern system is automated entire length from one panel

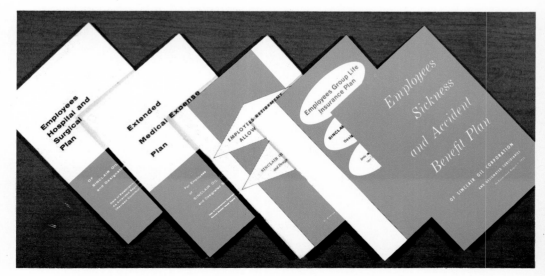

Sinclair and its operating companies contribute about $21 million a year to employee welfare benefits, nearly two percent of total operating revenue

1932: earliest ads were demure

SINCLAIR
OPALINE *and*
SINCLAIR PENNSYLVANIA
MOTOR OILS

Refined from older, finer crudes

SEE THE DEALER

1934: self-confident stance emerges

new SINCLAIR GASOLINE
HC

For performance..
No gasoline at regular price is superior to Sinclair H-C

1964: weather girl on TV, St. Louis

Sinclair

SINCLAIR OILS

COFFEYVILLE'S LARGEST DINNER BUCKET

1921: community identification antedated display advertising

1932: the original dinosaur, granddaddy of present Dino

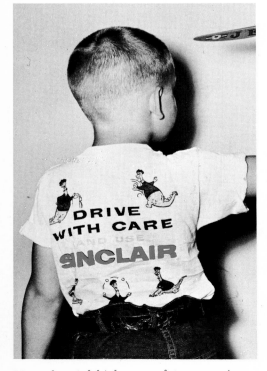

DRIVE WITH CARE AND USE SINCLAIR

Many-faceted highway safety campaign has earned public service accolades

WIN A CAR
a week

SINCLAIR 'RED' GRANGE FOOTBALL RADIO CONTEST

Entry Blanks Here

120 OTHER WEEKLY PRIZES

1936: national radio network invited fans to outguess Red Grange on scores

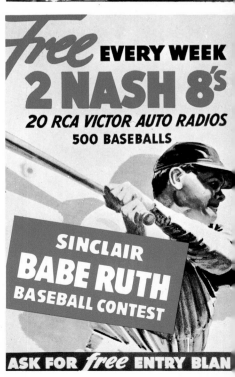

free **EVERY WEEK**
2 NASH 8's
20 RCA VICTOR AUTO RADIOS
500 BASEBALLS

SINCLAIR
BABE RUTH
BASEBALL CONTEST

ASK FOR *free* ENTRY BLAN

1937: another contest. Entry blanks were secured from service stations

1953: billboards plugged new product

personal service: since 1953 Al Ross typifies Sinclair at Princeton, N. J.

chapter 8:

public service
through advertising

Sinclair advertising has always been public service oriented. During the Chicago coal handlers strike of 1919, Mr. Sinclair set the principle (see page 26) that his corporate interests were inseparable from the public welfare. Since then some social concept has been inherent in most sales stimulants. The dinosaur trademark symbolizes a continuous educational program for conservation of natural resources, as part of Sinclair's own stewardship of oil reserves. A campaign to popularize America's national parks and monuments obviously encouraged gasoline sales from touring; it also won more than 60 national awards for public service by inculcating respect for the national heritage. A series exhorting visits to Civil War battlefields during the centennial received many prizes for sharpening the significances of America's past. With all this, Sinclair has sought the good will of the individual by attending his peculiar needs. Many promotions have been identified with the neighborhood dealer's relationship to patrons within driving range of his services. To inflate the tires of a boy's bicycle, to map a family vacation in a national park, to repair an oil burner on a cold night: these person-to-person exchanges help to build "a great name in oil."

great promotions stimulate buying public in many ways

Sinclair had little money to spend on advertising in its early days, or much need to publicize its wares in an expanding automotive economy in which demand often exceeded supply. Except for special appeals to farmers and the oil trade, media were unused until 1927, when five national magazines carried lubricant ads. In 1930 Sinclair turned to network radio with Phil Baker, telling women they would find service stations "as clean as your kitchen." With the dinosaur campaign of 1932, billings crossed $2 million for the first time, chiefly due to a minstrel show which rated among radio's "top ten" in popularity. Sinclair from 1934 was one of the first national marketers to use ads in movie houses. An antique car stamp album, similar to the dinosaur promotion of 1935, enlivened 1936 with 45 million giveaways.

Since World War II, heavy accent has been placed on news and weather shows pitched to specific localities, rather than shotgun-spread advertising to the entire national audience. The TV-radio pitch usually is specific. Give people an idea for a trip, and they'll probably take it, thus stimulating the entire oil industry. A "drive with care" promotion, which has included 10,000 exhortations on 880 radio and TV stations in a single year, has won the Alfred P. Sloan, Jr. award for public service advertising. Sinclair buys regional circulation in magazines, and TV-radio time precisely where Sinclair products are available, for greatest impact per dollar of cost.

1930s: big movie series lured farmers

1931: dealer did his own promotion

94

The SINCLAIR DINOSAUR BOOK

1934: *first booklet of Sinclair's outstanding educational program in paleontology and conservation, scientist-approved for use in schools*

Sinclair Dinosaur Stamp Album

BRONTOSAURUS

TYRANNOSAURUS

TRICERATOPS

Petroleum... Source of Fuels and Lubricants

1935: *this promotion stimulated national public interest in paleontology. Twelve weekly visits to stations were necessary to collect all the stamps*

public service takes many forms

A warm home...a warm friend

Dealer relationships begin early

Tanker crew rescues ditched airmen

Millionth visitors, N.Y. World's Fair

Shenandoah...

Conservation saved it for you. See it on your way to the New York World's Fair.

When you visit Shenandoah National Park and ride along the breathtaking Skyline Drive over the mountain tops, you will see a peak called Pollock's Knob, named for a man who looked beyond the years.

Thanks to George Freeman Pollock, future generations will see the Blue Ridge Mountains as the Indians and pioneers saw them, blazing with millions of wild flowers, forested with a hundred kind of trees, and watered by some of the clearest trout streams in America.

Pollock first saw Shenandoah's rolling ridges when he was a boy. For fifty years, he worked and fought to save the natural glory of this wilderness. Bit by bit, he bought and set aside mountain scenery. He walked the hillsides with governors, senators, businessmen, conservation-ists — anyone he could inspire with his dream.

Through his efforts, the Virginia Conservation and Economic Development Commission made a study. Local chambers of commerce helped. So did the Potomac Appalachian Trail Club. Some 24,000 Virginians pledged a million dollars. In 1927, Governor Harry F. Byrd signed a state appropriation for another million. And Shenandoah became *your* National Park.

Since then, our population has increased by 50 million. We need more Shenandoahs. We need more lands for outdoor recreation, so that more of our people will have the opportunity to know Nature's blessings and, through them, find refreshment of body and spirit. Everyone benefits from such conservation. That's why conservation is everyone's job.

Free tour service: If you are driving to the New York World's Fair, let Sinclair help plan your trip to include visits to Shenandoah or other National Parks. Write Tour Bureau, Sinclair Oil Building, 600 Fifth Avenue, New York, New York 10020.

Sinclair

A GREAT NAME IN OIL

Winner of sixty national awards and citations, series on conservation of natural resources exemplifies Sinclair emphasis on public service messages

chapter 9:

evolution of the company symbol

Industrial surveys repeatedly rank the Sinclair dinosaur as one of the most potent symbols of American business. Remarkably high percentages identify the dinosaur with Sinclair. This association is positive and pleasant. There is almost no confusion between Sinclair's Dino and other corporate trademarks. Marketing experts agree that the dinosaur is a "powerful unifying and associating concept." The connotation penetrates deeply: children are as fascinated with the pre-historic uniqueness of the dinosaurs as are adults, and the correlation with Sinclair therefore begins at an early age. Few trademarks can equal Dino's unique appeals.

Dinosaur has an infinite variety of good will uses. Above: an educational diorama from Sinclair exhibit, Chicago World's Fair of 1933. At right, a 1963 beach toy made from petrochemicals

identification with dinosaurs began in advertising of 1930

In 1930, Sinclair's advertising writers noted that Wellsville-refined lubricants—the best in the trade—derived from Pennsylvania grade crudes laid down more than 270 million years earlier. These oils were mellowing in the ground during the Mesozoic era when dinosaurs populated the earth. The obvious sales message was: the oldest crudes make the best oils. But how to dramatize this?

A series of advertisements in 104 newspapers and five national magazines featured a dozen of the strange dinosauri, from hideous-fanged tyrannosaurus rex and three-horned triceratops, to the unaggressive, vegetarian brontosaurus, a 40-ton lizard with neck and tail each 30 feet long. The campaign—confined entirely to Wellsville oils—was a great success. The curiosity value of it was tremendous.

But there was a significant and unexpected windfall. One of the dinosaurs generated a remarkable popular appeal, in fact was a real glamor boy: peace-loving but massive brontosaurus. The public equated him with power, endurance and stamina, the prime qualities of Sinclair products.

Without any particular promotion, the public accepted the brontosaurus affectionately as Sinclair's "Dino." He's been Dino ever since.

Earliest Sinclair brontosaurus was romanticized to curb reptile effect

1934: *the artistic Hogarth curve balance between head and tail begins to emerge, but Dino's body is ungainly; he still advertises only lubricants*

1936: *public's affectionate regard for Dino inspires series of humorous newspaper advertisements in which Sinclair, local dealer, split the cost*

1937: *fully aware now that brontosaurus has become a potent symbol, company extends his use to outdoor billboard advertising of its premium gasoline*

Chicago World's Fair exhibit 1933-1934 had 16 million viewers, featured seven life-size dinosaurs, two of which fought battle with horrendous sounds

1. This is Brontosaurus, the thunder reptile. He appears here to emphasize . . .

2. . . . the vast age of crude oils from which Sinclair Motor Oils are refined. Sinclair Opaline Motor Oil, for example, is refined from the oldest Mid-Continent crudes. These crudes were mellowing and filtering in the . . .

3. . . . earth even before dinosaurs roamed America. Oldest crudes plus most modern refining are the reasons why Opaline lasts longer and stands up better. Ask your nearby Sinclair dealer. You'll like the way he treats you.

1938: in magazine ads, same message as 1930 but brontosaurus alone used

Scholars accepted dinosaur promotions for school use with Sinclair's sponsorship, 1934-1938, of Dr. Barnum Brown's fossil-gathering expeditions

Containers used Dino in mid-1930s; note premium oil was mellowed longer

Dino becomes big star of ads, publicity and public identification

The dinosaur was such an instant hit with the public that in 1932 the Sinclair companies registered the brontosaurus as a trademark. By now P. G. Alen, creator of life-like papier-mache animals for motion pictures, was building a gigantic exhibit for the Century of Progress Exposition in Chicago. The authenticity of this display led to the first company-sponsored geological materials for schools, libraries and home study. These have been distributed by hundreds of thousands. To give academic stature to its promotions, Sinclair financed for several years the dinosaur-fossil search expeditions of Dr. Barnum Brown, then curator of fossil reptiles at the American Museum of Natural History. On Doctor Brown's death in January, 1963, Sinclair turned for scientific assistance to Dr. John H. Ostrom of Yale University's Peabody Museum of Natural History. He completed Doctor Brown's work as consultant on the paleontology exhibit at New York World's Fair in 1964.

Perhaps the Sinclair Refining Company's most successful single promotion was the issuance in 1935 of a dinosaur stamp album which could be filled only with colored dinosaur stamps issued one at a time weekly at service stations. The first printing of albums was distributed through dealers within 48 hours after a single network radio broadcast of the offer. The final totals were 4 million albums and 48 million stamps. During this period, company sales increased substantially.

1944: travelers saw Dino on display in New York's Grand Central Terminal

Dealers love Dino: Indianapolis, 1944

...Mount Holly, New Jersey, 1961, when gasoline was named Dino

1963: big publicity fanfare accompanied nine life-sized fiberglass dinosaurs barged 125 miles down Hudson River to site of New York World's Fair. Here: at tip of Manhattan

1964-65: nearly 10 million visitors jammed Sinclair's New York World's Fair pavilion; the star was Dino, who towered over a scientifically-accurate re-enactment of earth life during Mesozoic age

Dino is known world-widely: on tanks

...on company tankers

...on products containers

chapter 10:

toward tomorrow

The success of Mr. Steiniger's 1-2-3 profit program caused management to raise its sights on future earnings. Corporate objectives for the five years 1966-70 are established at specific advancing profit goals which are expected to be met. Gradually the long-sought goals are being realized: a thrust toward parity of crude oil production with refinery throughput; less dependence on gasoline pricing for profit; stabilizing diversification in chemicals; expanding foreign production and marketing operations; and increased natural gas production. All these programs are accompanied by higher operating efficiency, and by deep slashes in expenses. Five-year projections foresee doubled revenues from petrochemicals, improved margins for petroleum products due to further quality upgrading, and additional economies from the momentum of cost-cutting programs already in effect. 🦕 🦕 Nothing succeeds like success. As the three-pronged program is reflected in rising earnings, each Sinclair man and woman finds a new significance in the daily job, and a renewed determination to make further contributions to Sinclair's accelerating progress. 🦕 🦕 At its Fiftieth Anniversary, Sinclair's management looks forward to a golden future rather than back wistfully at its colorful past.

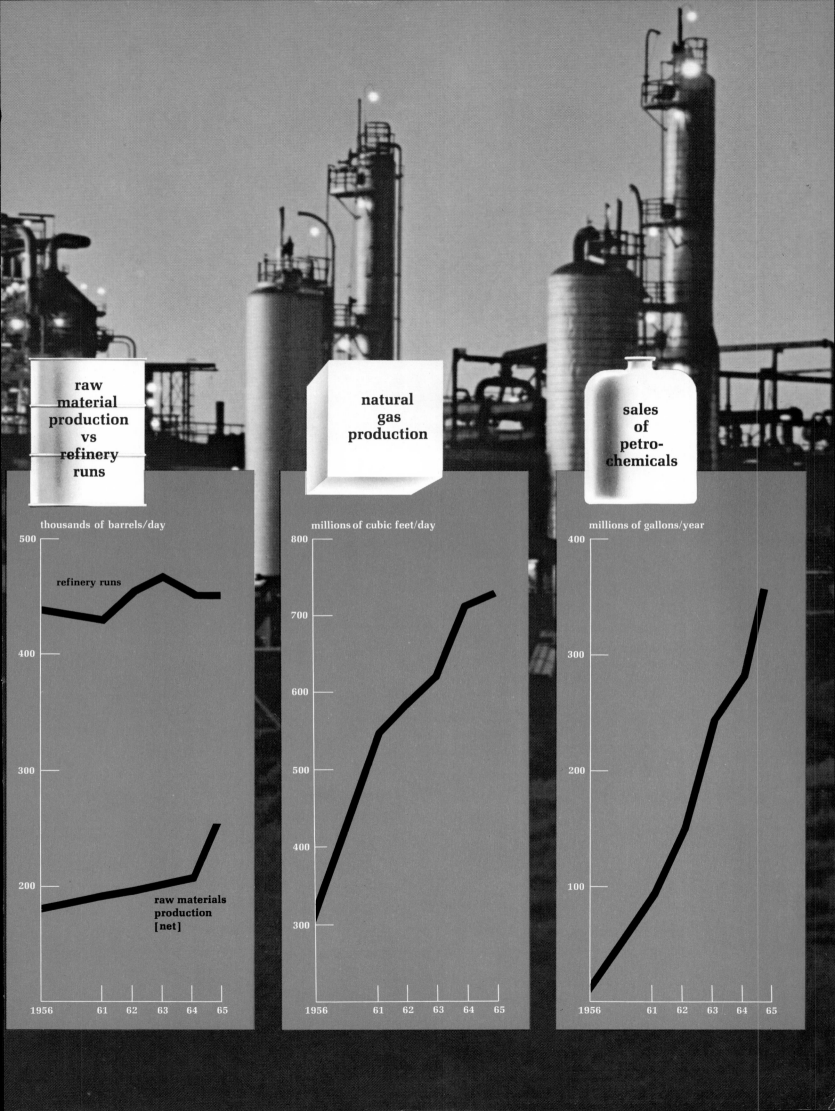

raw material production vs refinery runs

thousands of barrels/day

500

refinery runs

400

300

200

raw materials production [net]

1956   61   62   63   64   65

natural gas production

millions of cubic feet/day

800

700

600

500

400

300

1956   61   62   63   64   65

sales of petro-chemicals

millions of gallons/year

400

300

200

100

1956   61   62   63   64   65

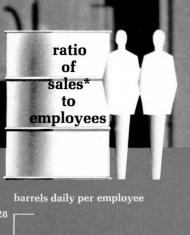

ratio
of
sales*
to
employees

investment
per
employee

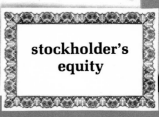

stockholder's
equity

barrels daily per employee

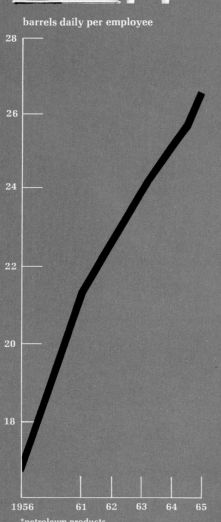

28

26

24

22

20

18

1956   61   62   63   64   65

*petroleum products

thousands of dollars

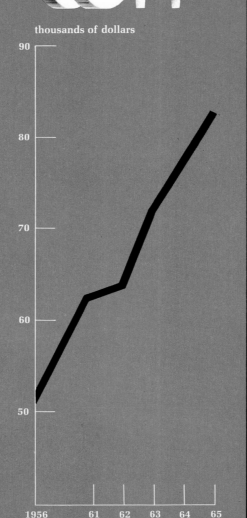

90

80

70

60

50

1956   61   62   63   64   65

millions of dollars

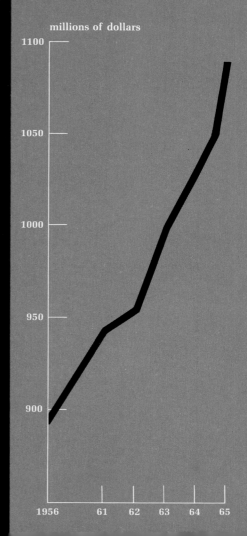

1100

1050

1000

950

900

1956   61   62   63   64   65